nickelodeon™

降击神通

AVATAR

THE LAST AIRBENDER™

Created by
Bryan Konietzko
Michael Dante DiMartino

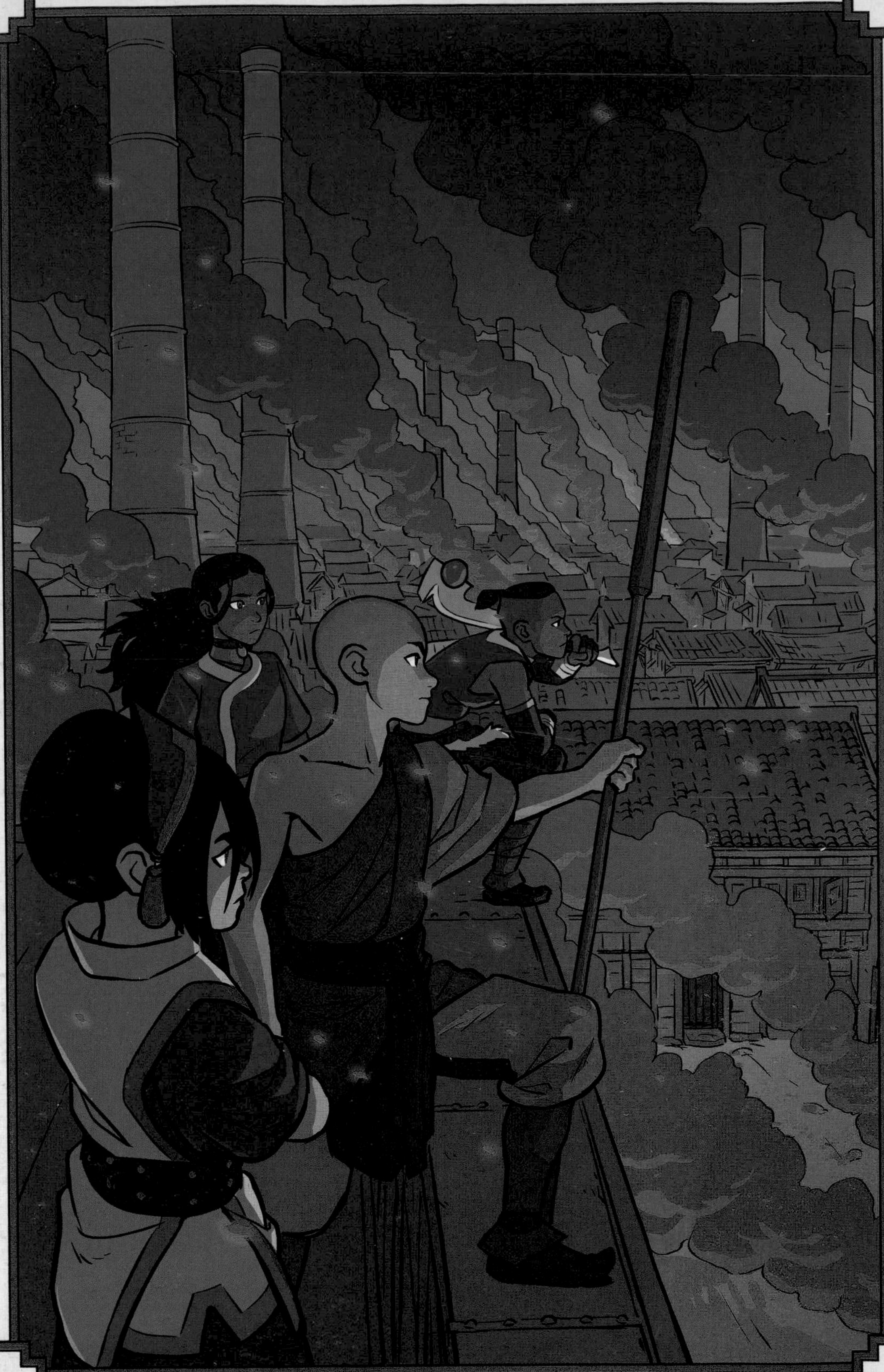

nickelodeon

降去神通

AVATAR

THE LAST AIRBENDER™

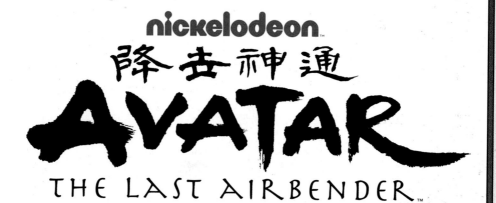

IMBALANCE • PART THREE

script
FAITH ERIN HICKS

art
PETER WARTMAN

colors
ADELE MATERA

lettering
RICHARD STARKINGS & COMICRAFT'S JIMMY BETANCOURT

cover
PETER WARTMAN with **RYAN HILL**

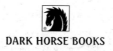

DARK HORSE BOOKS

president and publisher
MIKE RICHARDSON

editor
RACHEL ROBERTS

assistant editor
JENNY BLENK

collection designer
SARAH TERRY

digital art technician
CHRISTIANNE GILLENARDO-GOUDREAU

martial arts consultant and model
TODD BALTHAZOR

Special thanks to Linda Lee, James Salerno, and Joan Hilty at Nickelodeon,
and to Bryan Konietzko, Michael Dante DiMartino, and Tim Hedrick.

Published by **Dark Horse Books**
A division of Dark Horse Comics LLC
10956 SE Main Street, Milwaukie, OR 97222

DarkHorse.com
Nick.com

To find a comics shop in your area, visit comicshoplocator.com

First edition: October 2019 | ISBN 978-1-50670-813-3

1 3 5 7 9 10 8 6 4 2
Printed in China

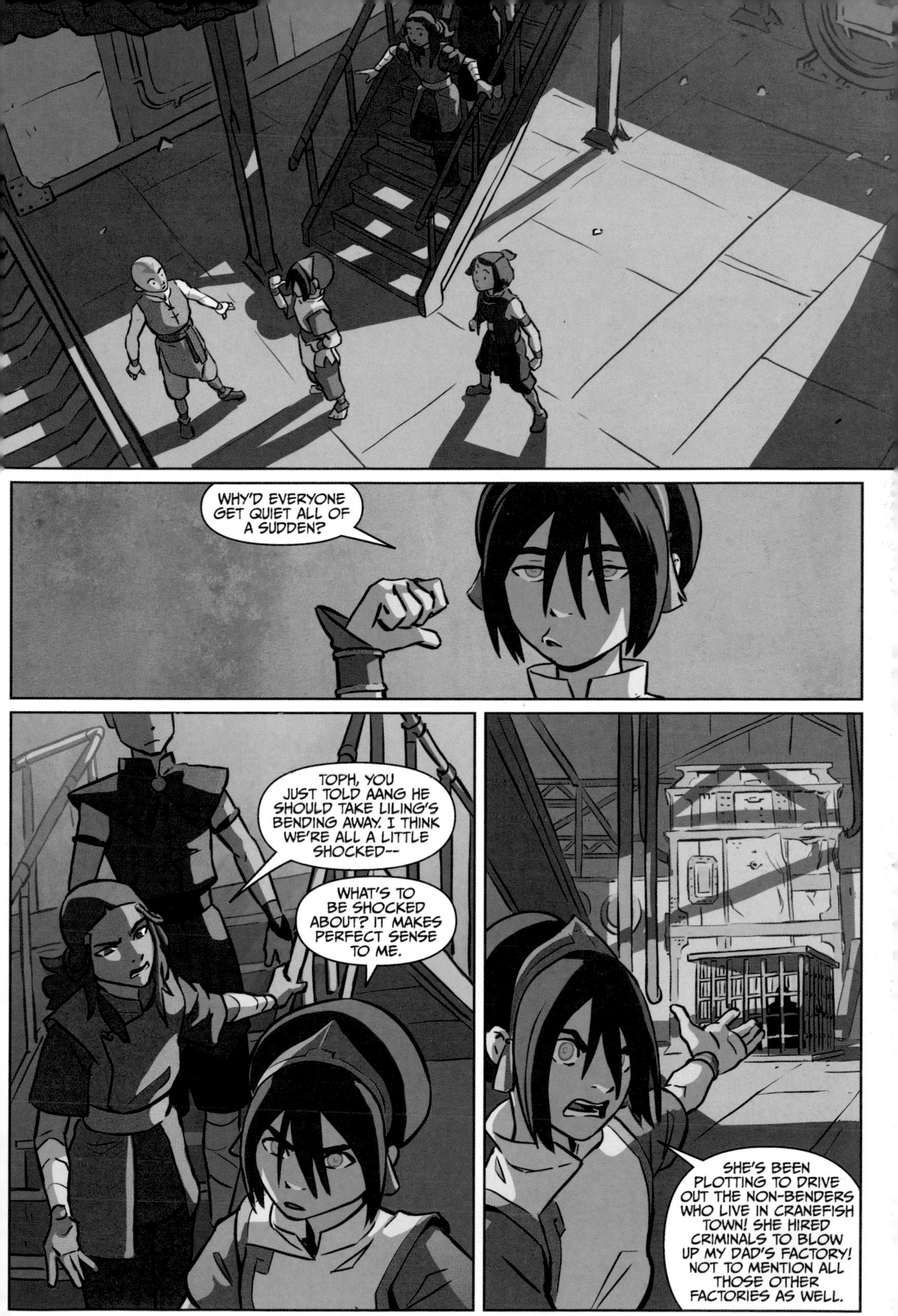
WHY'D EVERYONE GET QUIET ALL OF A SUDDEN?
TOPH, YOU JUST TOLD AANG HE SHOULD TAKE LILING'S BENDING AWAY. I THINK WE'RE ALL A LITTLE SHOCKED--
WHAT'S TO BE SHOCKED ABOUT? IT MAKES PERFECT SENSE TO ME.
SHE'S BEEN PLOTTING TO DRIVE OUT THE NON-BENDERS WHO LIVE IN CRANEFISH TOWN! SHE HIRED CRIMINALS TO BLOW UP MY DAD'S FACTORY! NOT TO MENTION ALL THOSE OTHER FACTORIES AS WELL.

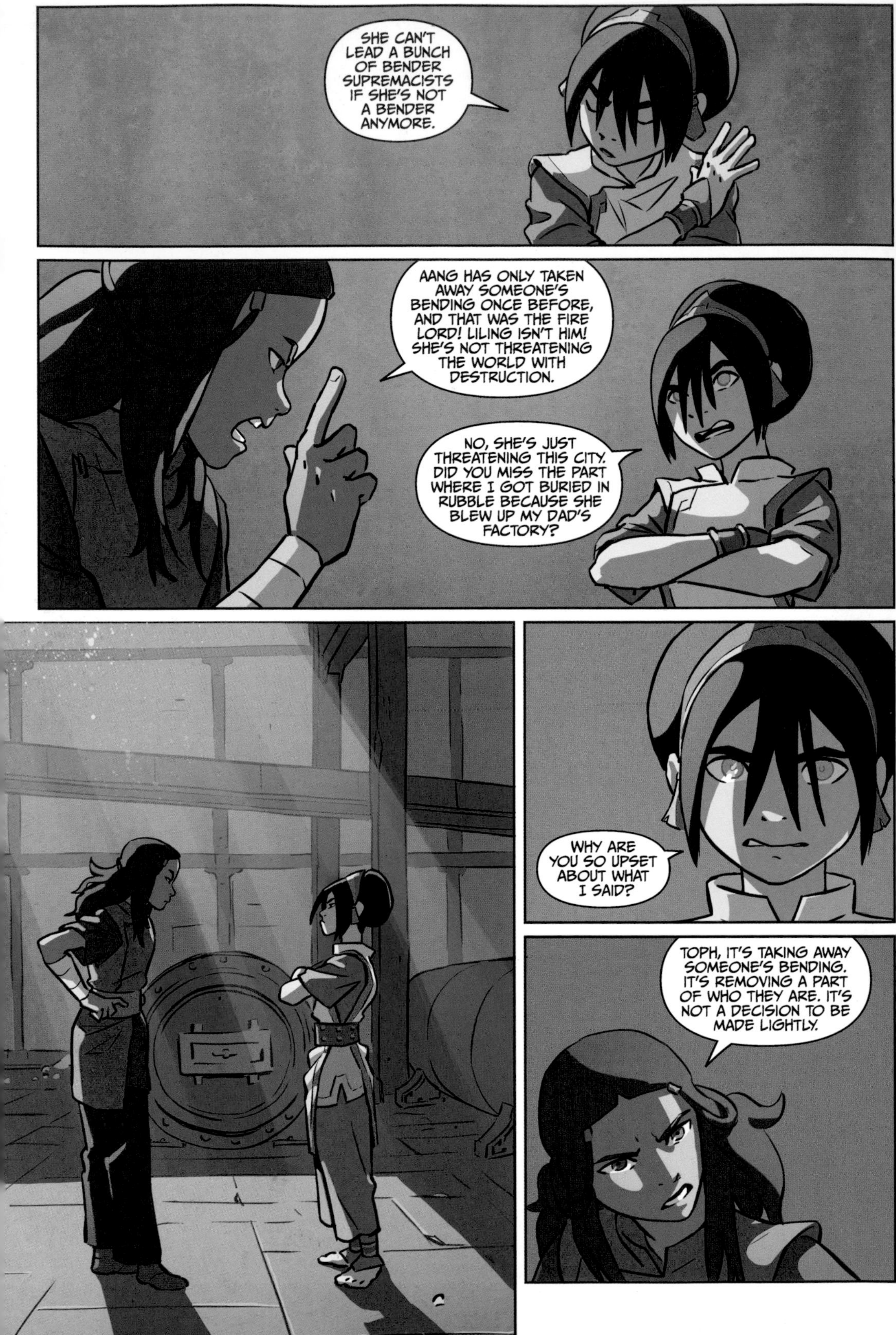
SHE CAN'T LEAD A BUNCH OF BENDER SUPREMACISTS IF SHE'S NOT A BENDER ANYMORE.
AANG HAS ONLY TAKEN AWAY SOMEONE'S BENDING ONCE BEFORE, AND THAT WAS THE FIRE LORD! LILING ISN'T HIM! SHE'S NOT THREATENING THE WORLD WITH DESTRUCTION.
NO, SHE'S JUST THREATENING THIS CITY. DID YOU MISS THE PART WHERE I GOT BURIED IN RUBBLE BECAUSE SHE BLEW UP MY DAD'S FACTORY?
WHY ARE YOU SO UPSET ABOUT WHAT I SAID?
TOPH, IT'S TAKING AWAY SOMEONE'S BENDING. IT'S REMOVING A PART OF WHO THEY ARE. IT'S NOT A DECISION TO BE MADE LIGHTLY.

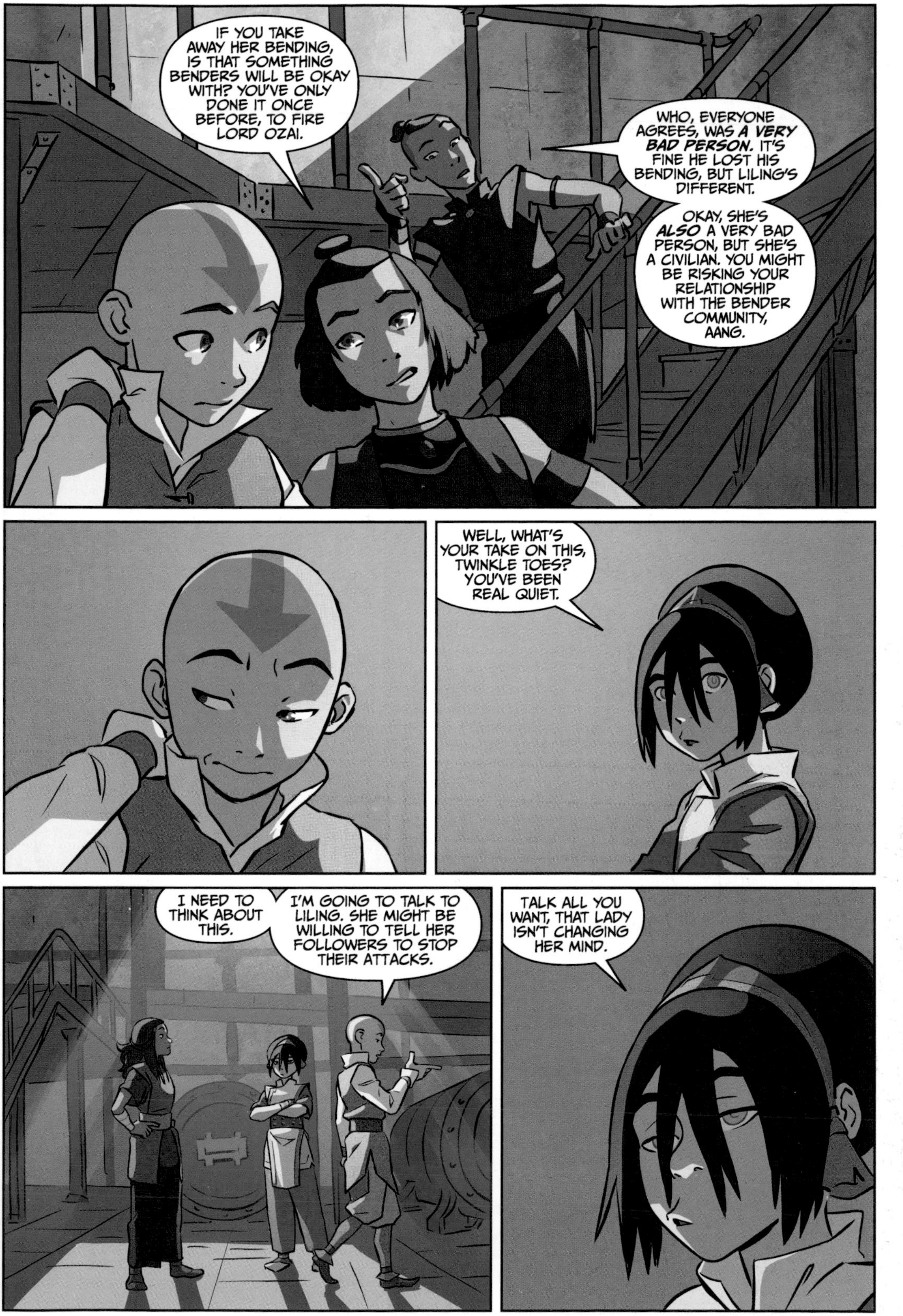
IF YOU TAKE AWAY HER BENDING, IS THAT SOMETHING BENDERS WILL BE OKAY WITH? YOU'VE ONLY DONE IT ONCE BEFORE, TO FIRE LORD OZAI.
WHO, EVERYONE AGREES, WAS ***A VERY BAD PERSON.*** IT'S FINE HE LOST HIS BENDING, BUT LILING'S DIFFERENT.
OKAY, SHE'S ***ALSO*** A VERY BAD PERSON, BUT SHE'S A CIVILIAN. YOU MIGHT BE RISKING YOUR RELATIONSHIP WITH THE BENDER COMMUNITY, AANG.
WELL, WHAT'S YOUR TAKE ON THIS, TWINKLE TOES? YOU'VE BEEN REAL QUIET.
I NEED TO THINK ABOUT THIS.
I'M GOING TO TALK TO LILING. SHE MIGHT BE WILLING TO TELL HER FOLLOWERS TO STOP THEIR ATTACKS.
TALK ALL YOU WANT, THAT LADY ISN'T CHANGING HER MIND.

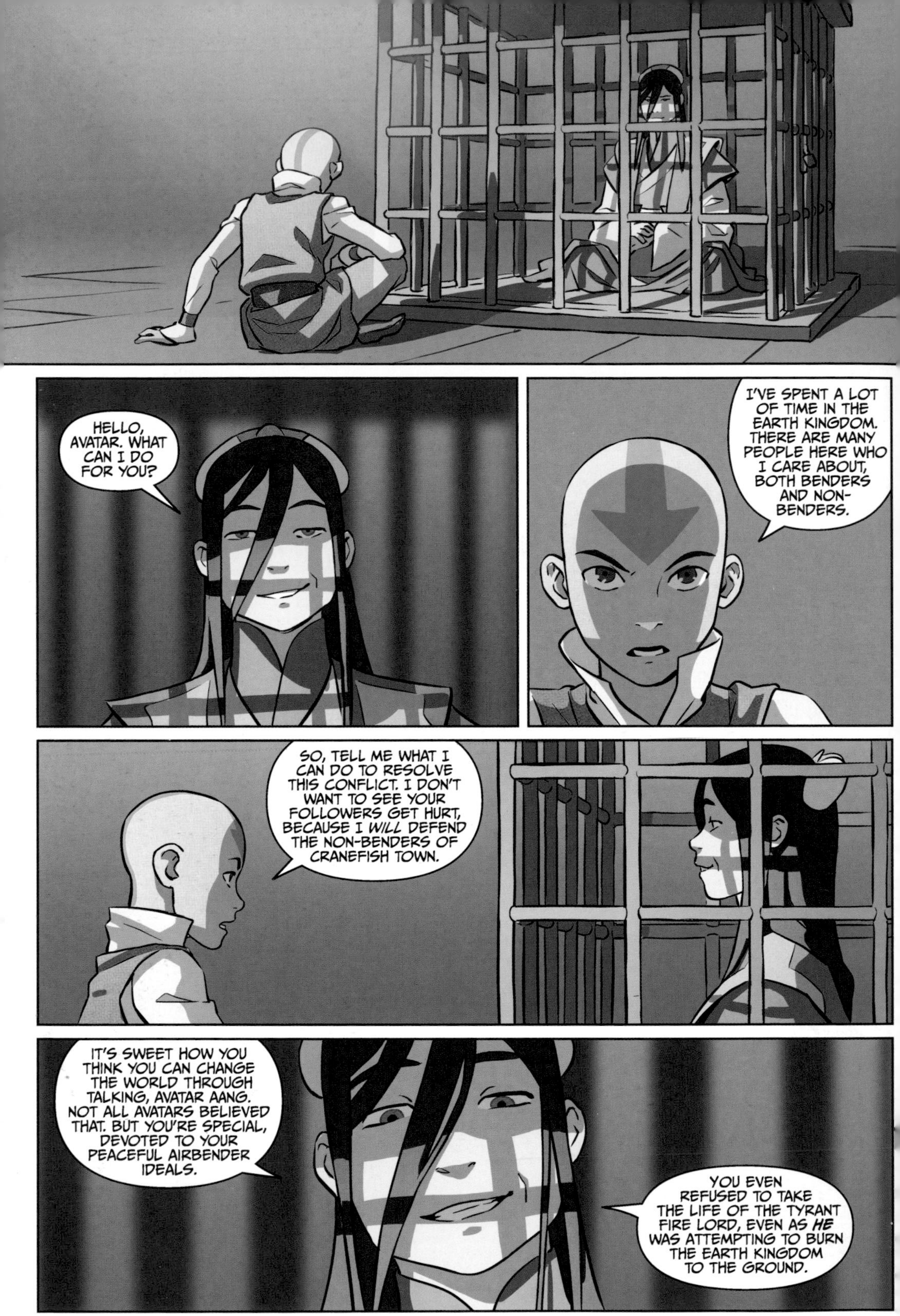
HELLO, AVATAR. WHAT CAN I DO FOR YOU?
I'VE SPENT A LOT OF TIME IN THE EARTH KINGDOM. THERE ARE MANY PEOPLE HERE WHO I CARE ABOUT, BOTH BENDERS AND NON-BENDERS.
SO, TELL ME WHAT I CAN DO TO RESOLVE THIS CONFLICT. I DON'T WANT TO SEE YOUR FOLLOWERS GET HURT, BECAUSE I *WILL* DEFEND THE NON-BENDERS OF CRANEFISH TOWN.
IT'S SWEET HOW YOU THINK YOU CAN CHANGE THE WORLD THROUGH TALKING, AVATAR AANG. NOT ALL AVATARS BELIEVED THAT. BUT YOU'RE SPECIAL, DEVOTED TO YOUR PEACEFUL AIRBENDER IDEALS.
YOU EVEN REFUSED TO TAKE THE LIFE OF THE TYRANT FIRE LORD, EVEN AS ***HE*** WAS ATTEMPTING TO BURN THE EARTH KINGDOM TO THE GROUND.

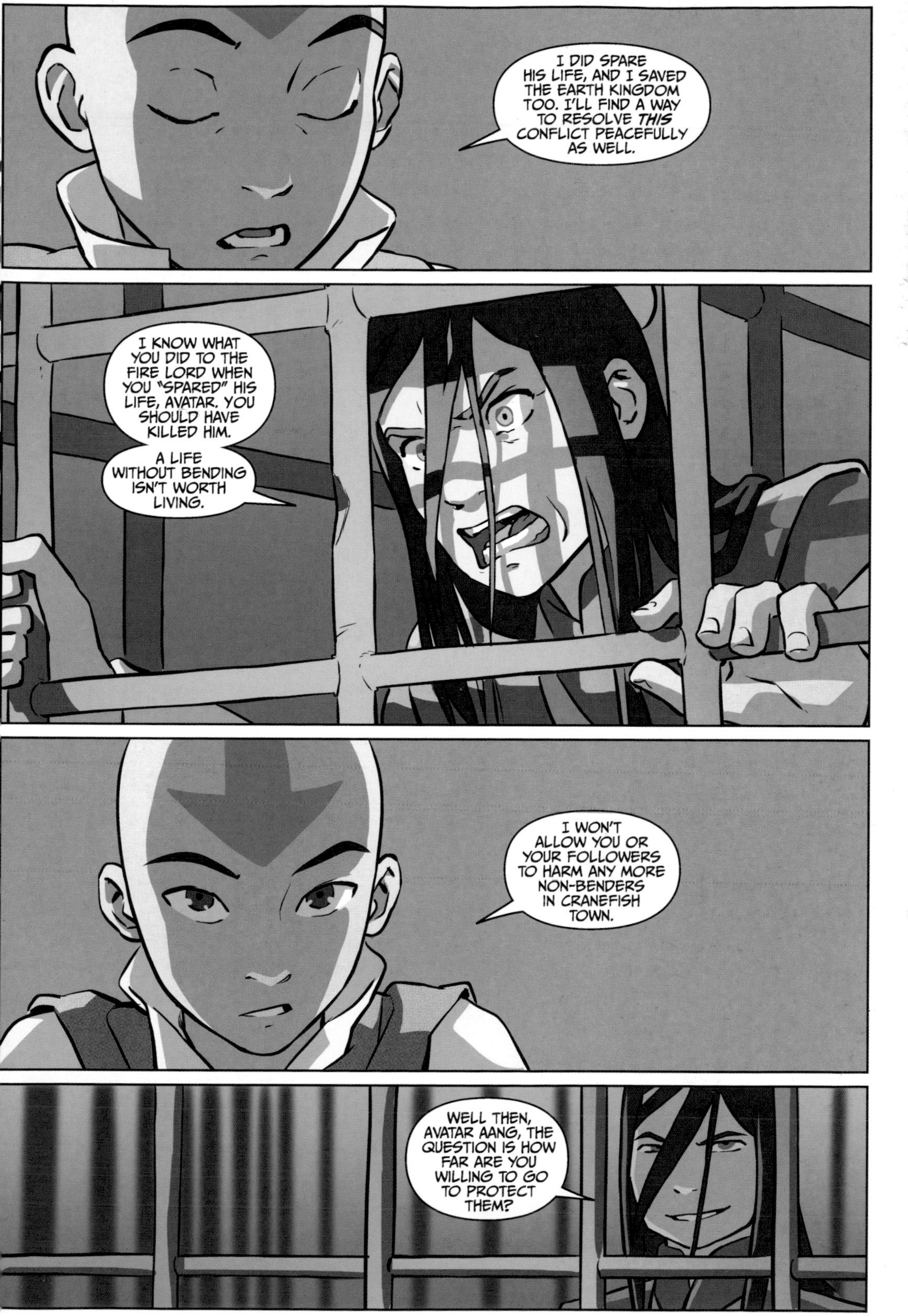
I DID SPARE HIS LIFE, AND I SAVED THE EARTH KINGDOM TOO. I'LL FIND A WAY TO RESOLVE *THIS* CONFLICT PEACEFULLY AS WELL.
I KNOW WHAT YOU DID TO THE FIRE LORD WHEN YOU "SPARED" HIS LIFE, AVATAR. YOU SHOULD HAVE KILLED HIM.
A LIFE WITHOUT BENDING ISN'T WORTH LIVING.
I WON'T ALLOW YOU OR YOUR FOLLOWERS TO HARM ANY MORE NON-BENDERS IN CRANEFISH TOWN.
WELL THEN, AVATAR AANG, THE QUESTION IS HOW FAR ARE YOU WILLING TO GO TO PROTECT THEM?

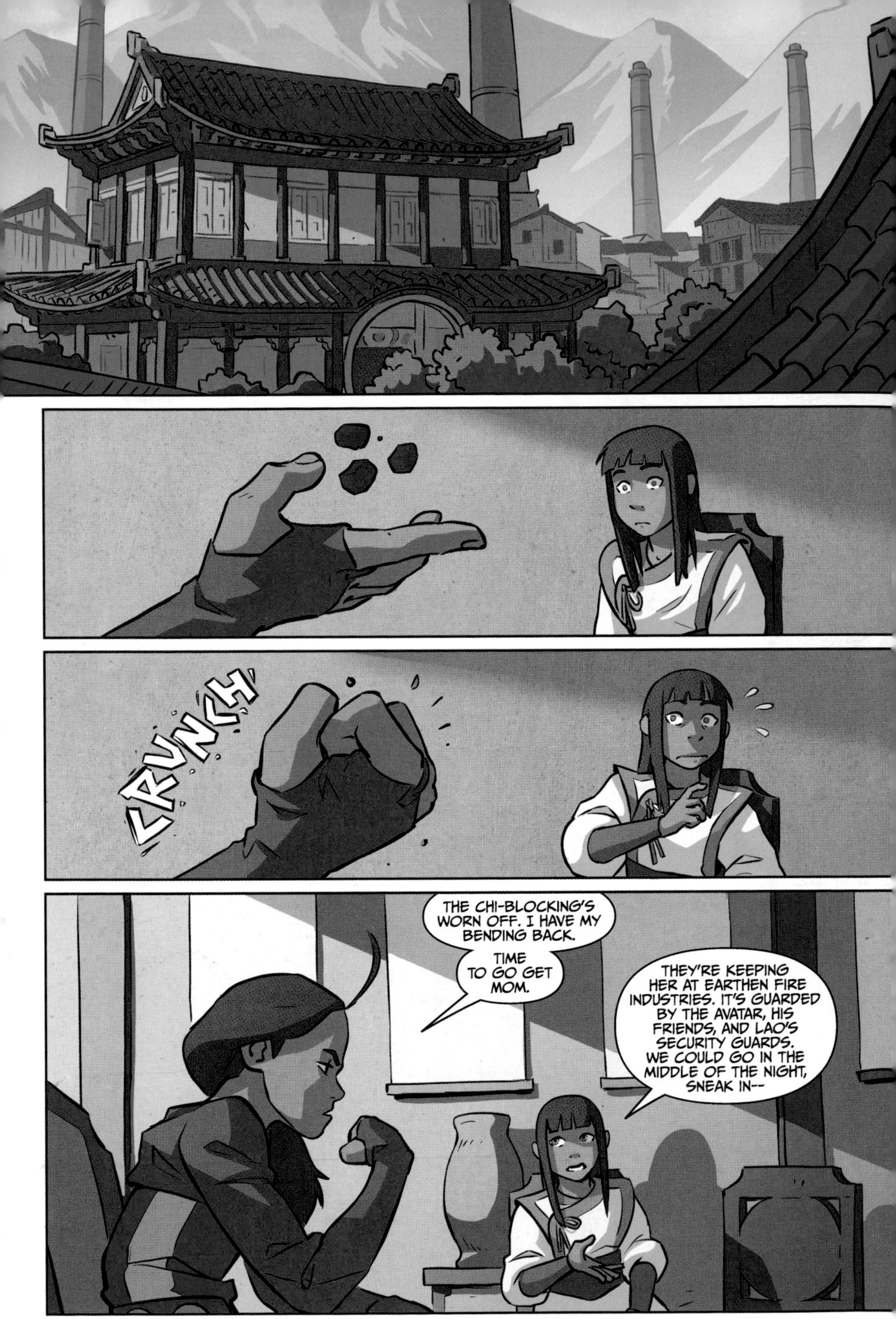
CRUNCH
THE CHI-BLOCKING'S WORN OFF. I HAVE MY BENDING BACK.
TIME TO GO GET MOM.
THEY'RE KEEPING HER AT EARTHEN FIRE INDUSTRIES. IT'S GUARDED BY THE AVATAR, HIS FRIENDS, AND LAO'S SECURITY GUARDS. WE COULD GO IN THE MIDDLE OF THE NIGHT, SNEAK IN--

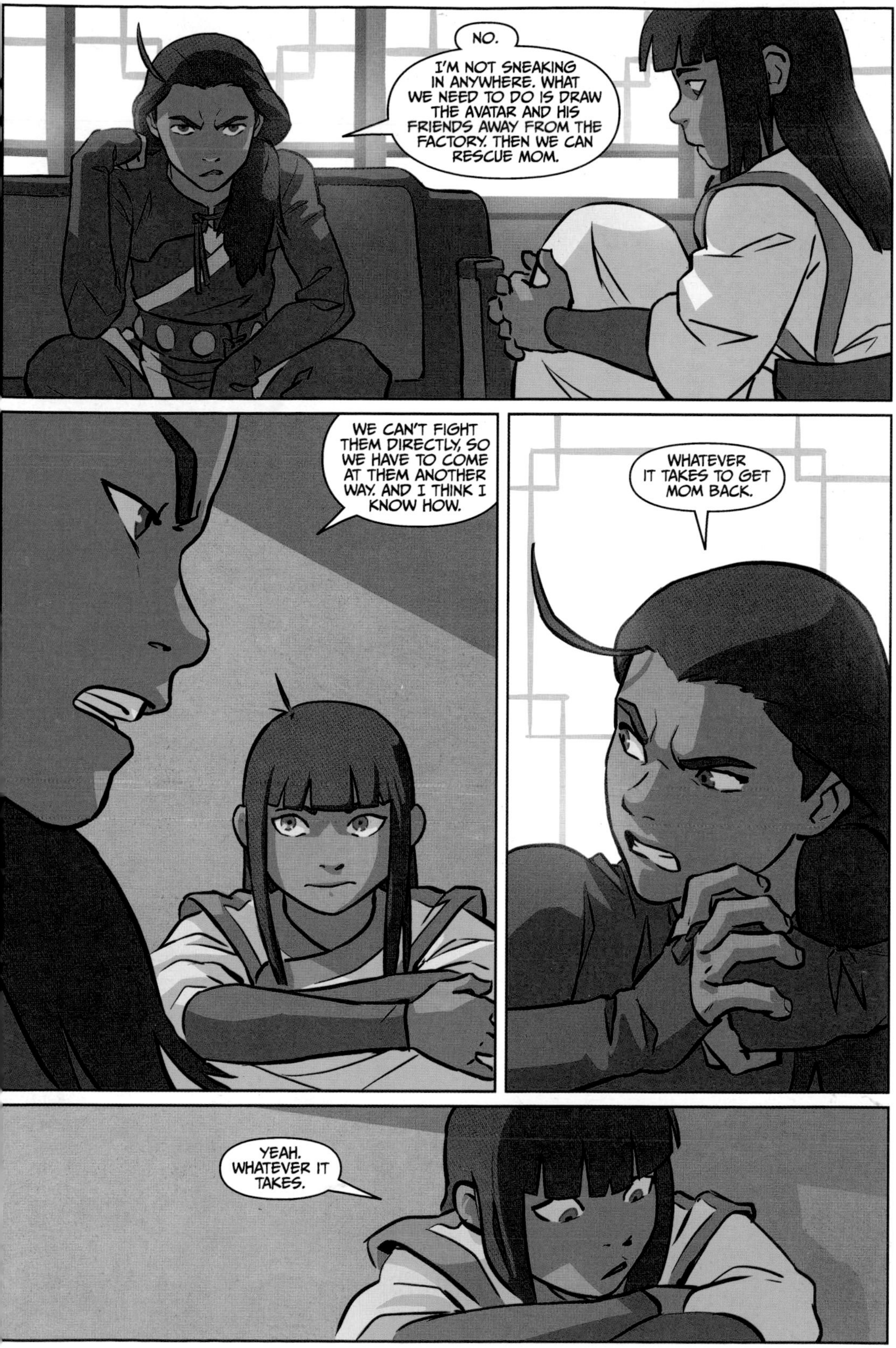
NO.
I'M NOT SNEAKING IN ANYWHERE. WHAT WE NEED TO DO IS DRAW THE AVATAR AND HIS FRIENDS AWAY FROM THE FACTORY. THEN WE CAN RESCUE MOM.
WE CAN'T FIGHT THEM DIRECTLY, SO WE HAVE TO COME AT THEM ANOTHER WAY. AND I THINK I KNOW HOW.
WHATEVER IT TAKES TO GET MOM BACK.
YEAH. WHATEVER IT TAKES.

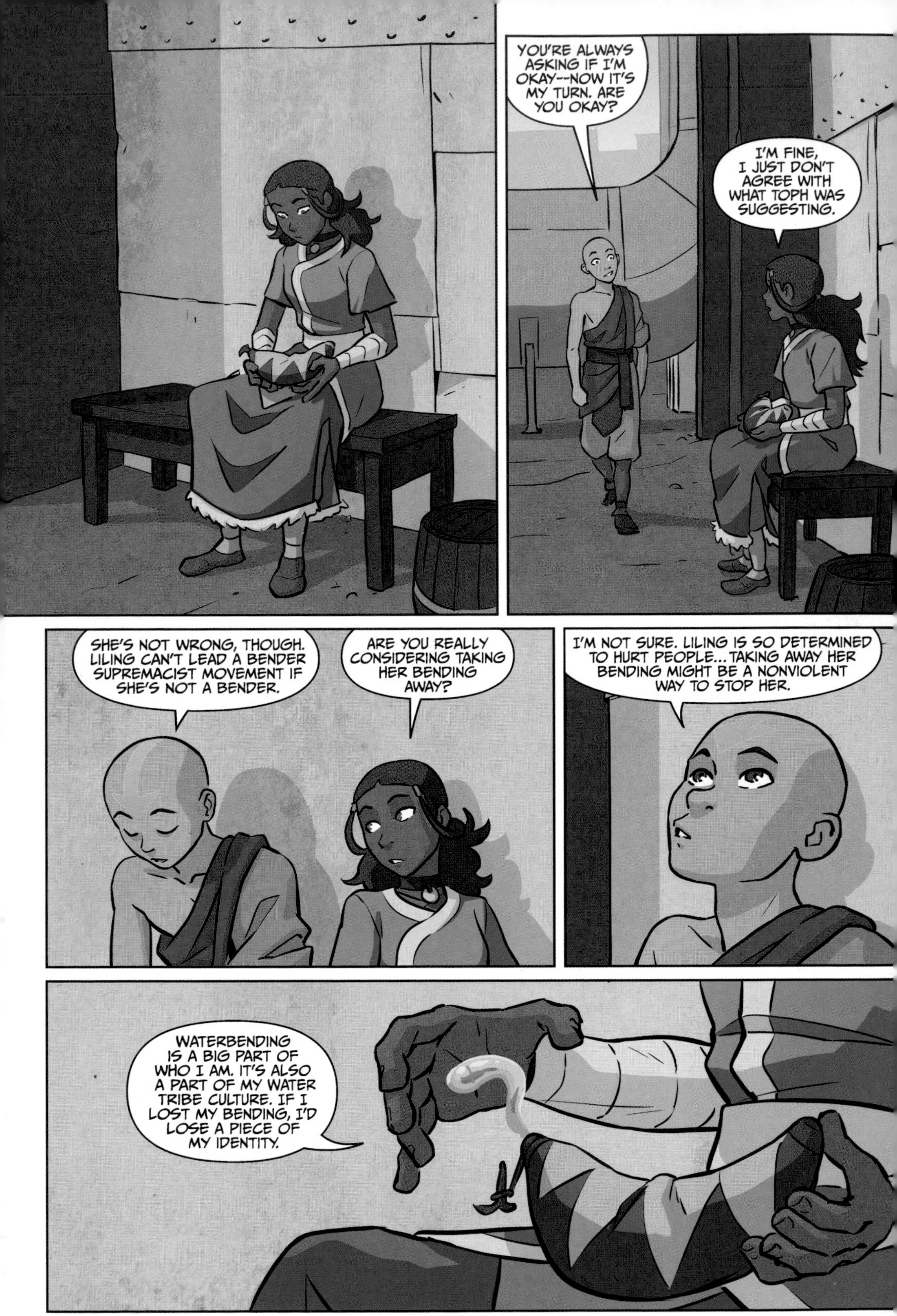
YOU'RE ALWAYS ASKING IF I'M OKAY--NOW IT'S MY TURN. ARE YOU OKAY?
I'M FINE, I JUST DON'T AGREE WITH WHAT TOPH WAS SUGGESTING.
SHE'S NOT WRONG, THOUGH. LILING CAN'T LEAD A BENDER SUPREMACIST MOVEMENT IF SHE'S NOT A BENDER.
ARE YOU REALLY CONSIDERING TAKING HER BENDING AWAY?
I'M NOT SURE. LILING IS SO DETERMINED TO HURT PEOPLE... TAKING AWAY HER BENDING MIGHT BE A NONVIOLENT WAY TO STOP HER.
WATERBENDING IS A BIG PART OF WHO I AM. IT'S ALSO A PART OF MY WATER TRIBE CULTURE. IF I LOST MY BENDING, I'D LOSE A PIECE OF MY IDENTITY.

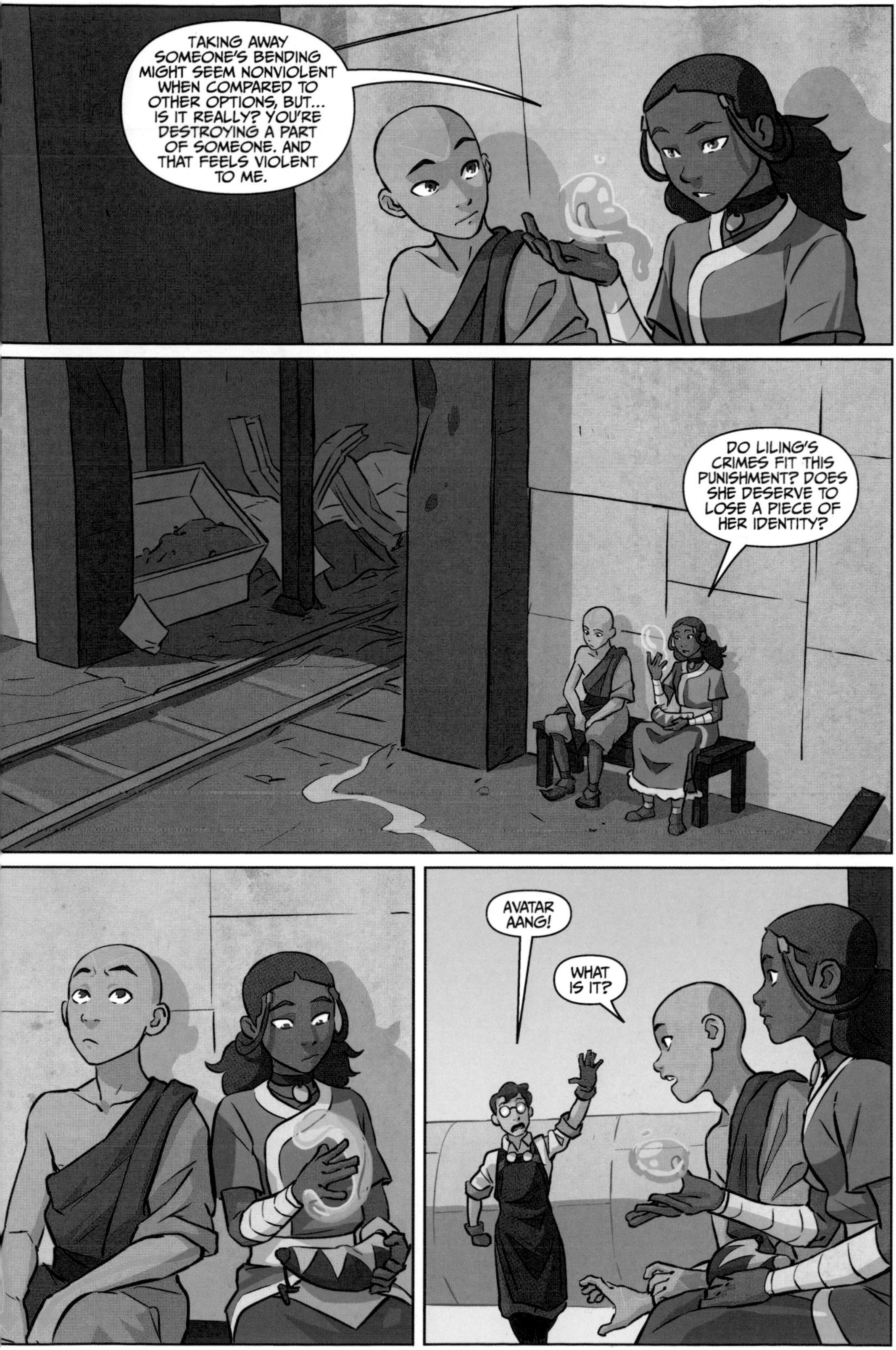
TAKING AWAY SOMEONE'S BENDING MIGHT SEEM NONVIOLENT WHEN COMPARED TO OTHER OPTIONS, BUT... IS IT REALLY? YOU'RE DESTROYING A PART OF SOMEONE. AND THAT FEELS VIOLENT TO ME.
DO LILING'S CRIMES FIT THIS PUNISHMENT? DOES SHE DESERVE TO LOSE A PIECE OF HER IDENTITY?
AVATAR AANG!
WHAT IS IT?

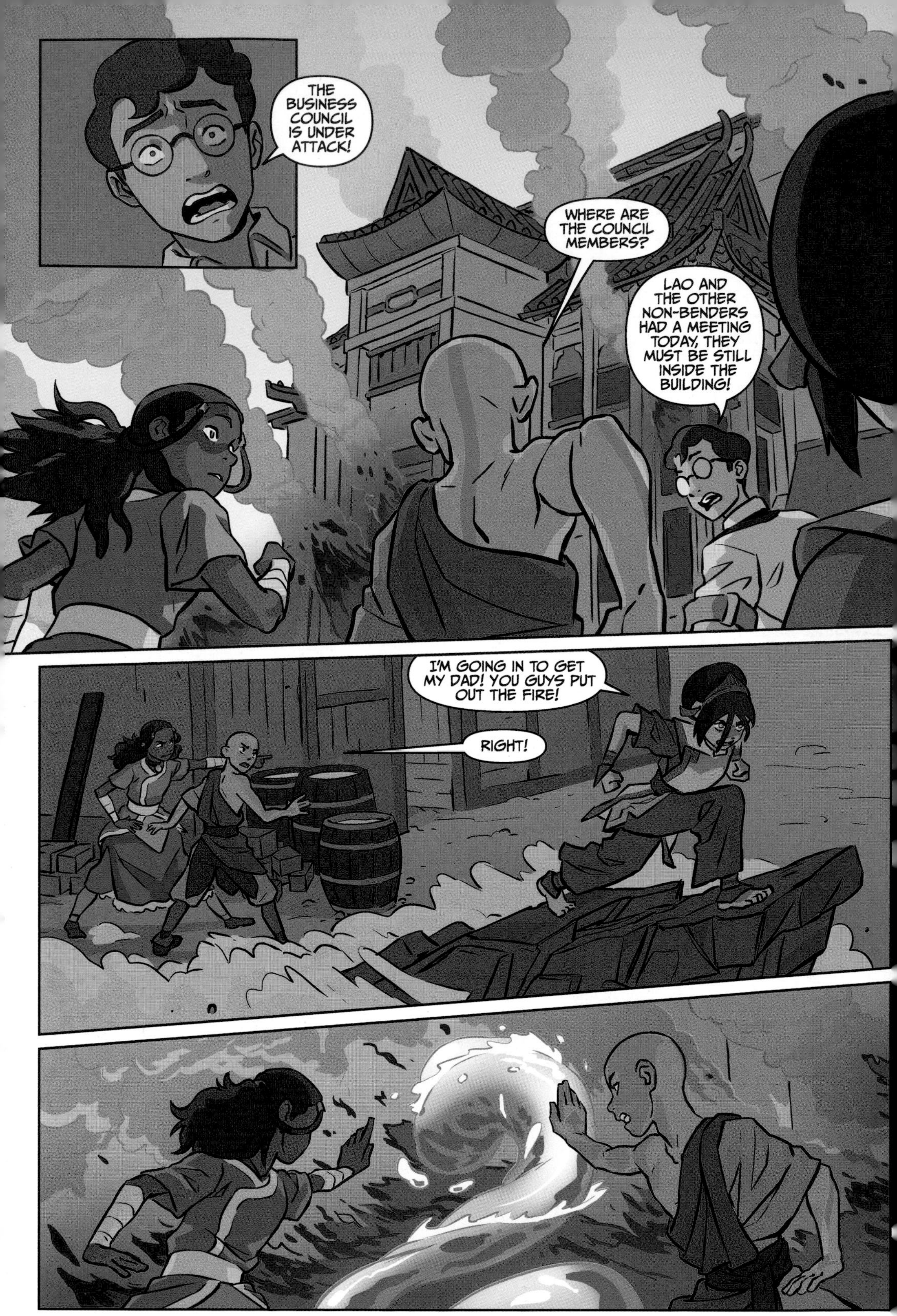
THE BUSINESS COUNCIL IS UNDER ATTACK!
WHERE ARE THE COUNCIL MEMBERS?
LAO AND THE OTHER NON-BENDERS HAD A MEETING TODAY, THEY MUST BE STILL INSIDE THE BUILDING!
I'M GOING IN TO GET MY DAD! YOU GUYS PUT OUT THE FIRE!
RIGHT!

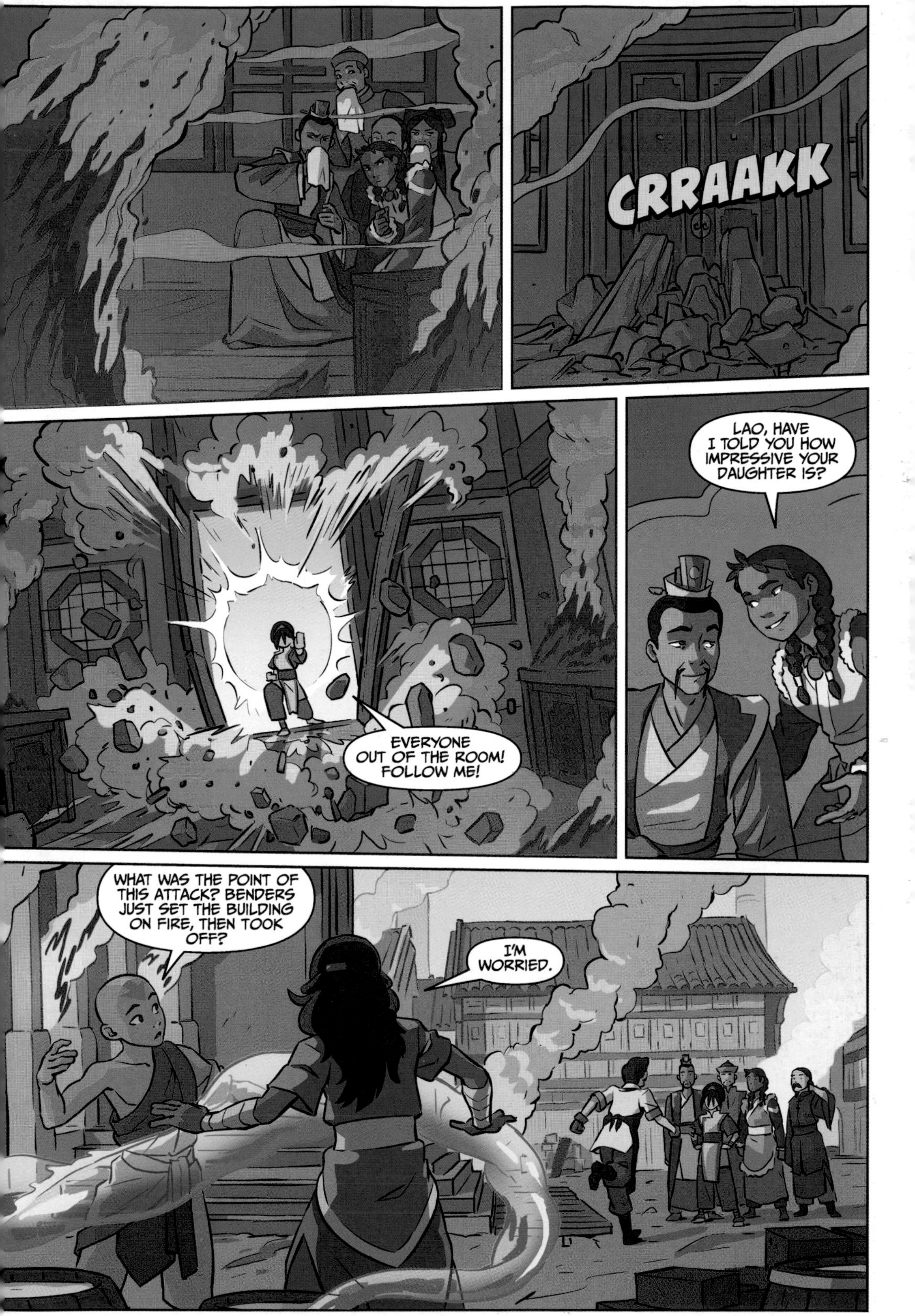
CRRAAKK
EVERYONE OUT OF THE ROOM! FOLLOW ME!
LAO, HAVE I TOLD YOU HOW IMPRESSIVE YOUR DAUGHTER IS?
WHAT WAS THE POINT OF THIS ATTACK? BENDERS JUST SET THE BUILDING ON FIRE, THEN TOOK OFF?
I'M WORRIED.

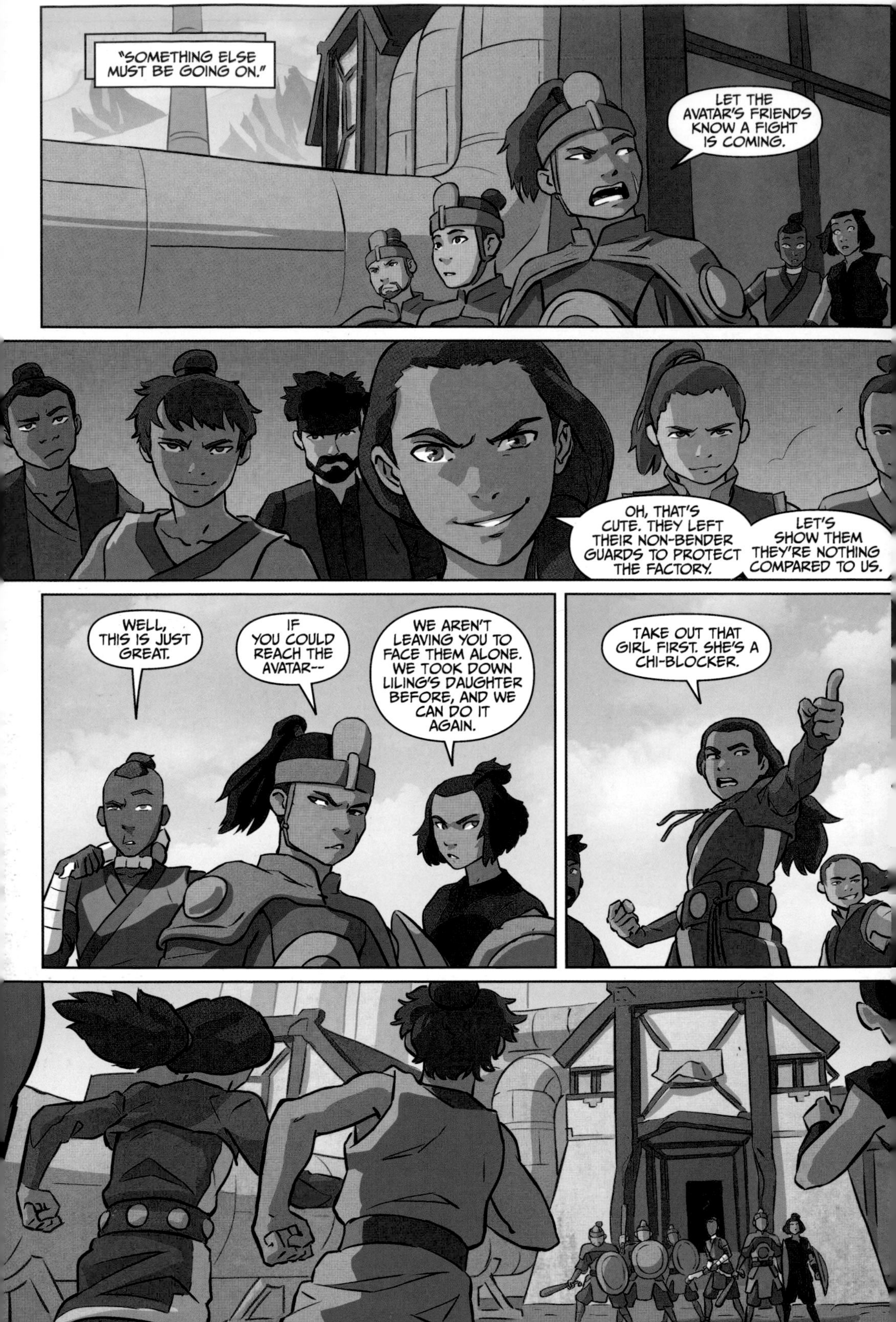
"SOMETHING ELSE MUST BE GOING ON."
LET THE AVATAR'S FRIENDS KNOW A FIGHT IS COMING.
OH, THAT'S CUTE. THEY LEFT THEIR NON-BENDER GUARDS TO PROTECT THE FACTORY.
LET'S SHOW THEM THEY'RE NOTHING COMPARED TO US.
WELL, THIS IS JUST GREAT.
IF YOU COULD REACH THE AVATAR--
WE AREN'T LEAVING YOU TO FACE THEM ALONE. WE TOOK DOWN LILING'S DAUGHTER BEFORE, AND WE CAN DO IT AGAIN.
TAKE OUT THAT GIRL FIRST. SHE'S A CHI-BLOCKER.

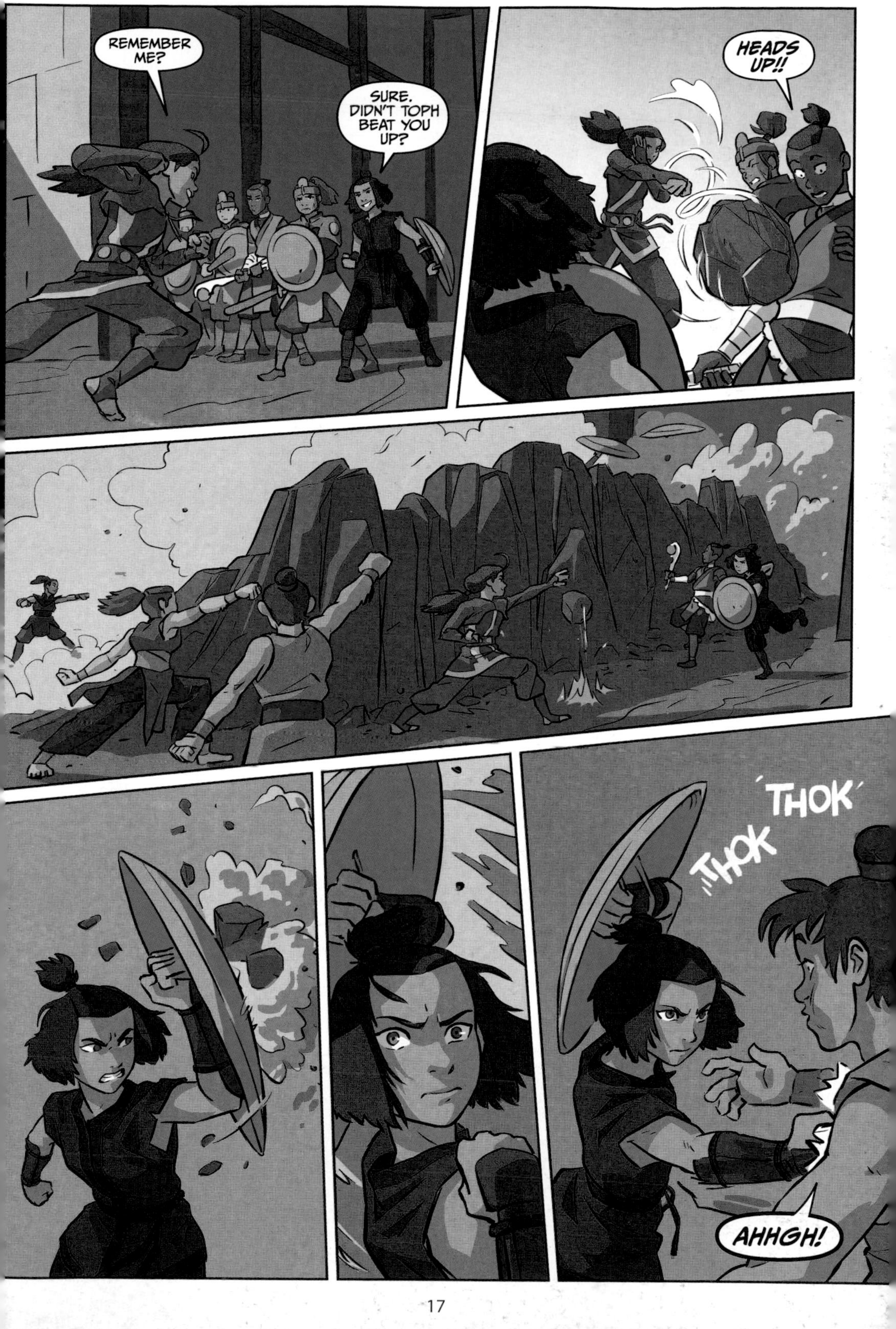
REMEMBER ME?
SURE. DIDN'T TOPH BEAT YOU UP?
HEADS UP!!
THOK
THOK
AHHGH!

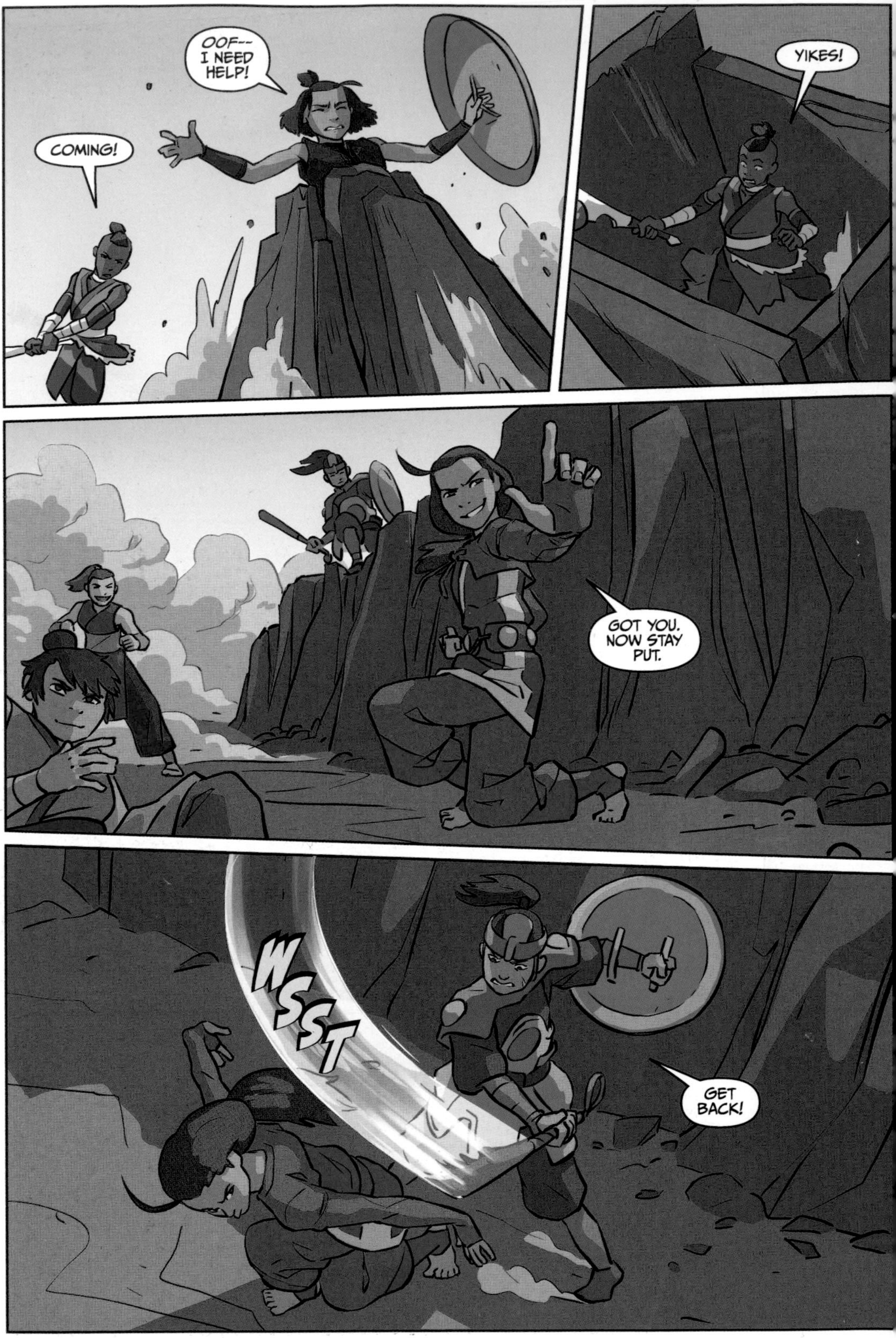
OOF--
I NEED
HELP!
COMING!
YIKES!
GOT YOU.
NOW STAY
PUT.
WSST
GET
BACK!

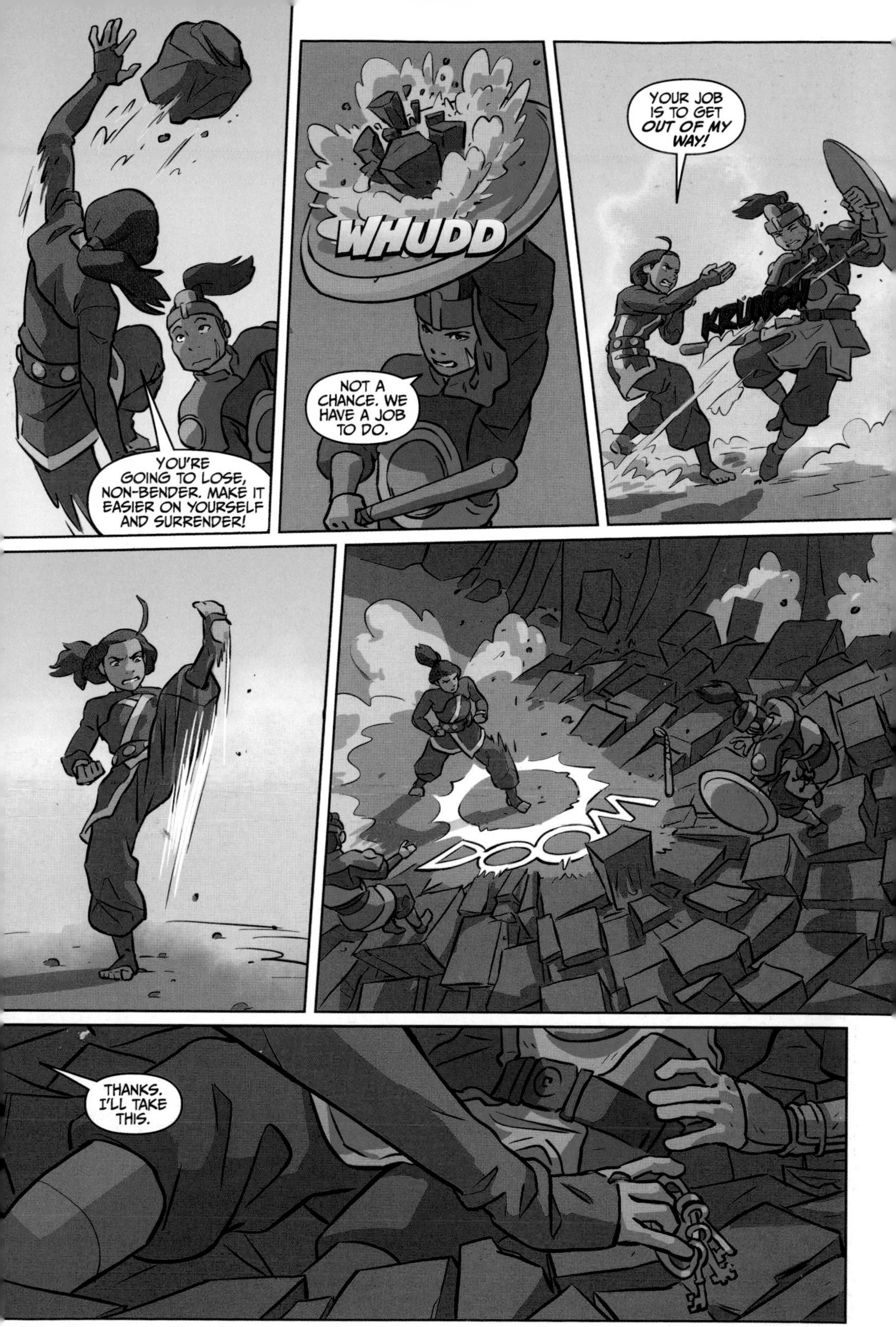
YOU'RE GOING TO LOSE, NON-BENDER. MAKE IT EASIER ON YOURSELF AND SURRENDER!
WHUDD
NOT A CHANCE. WE HAVE A JOB TO DO.
YOUR JOB IS TO GET OUT OF MY WAY!
KRUNCH
DOOM
THANKS. I'LL TAKE THIS.

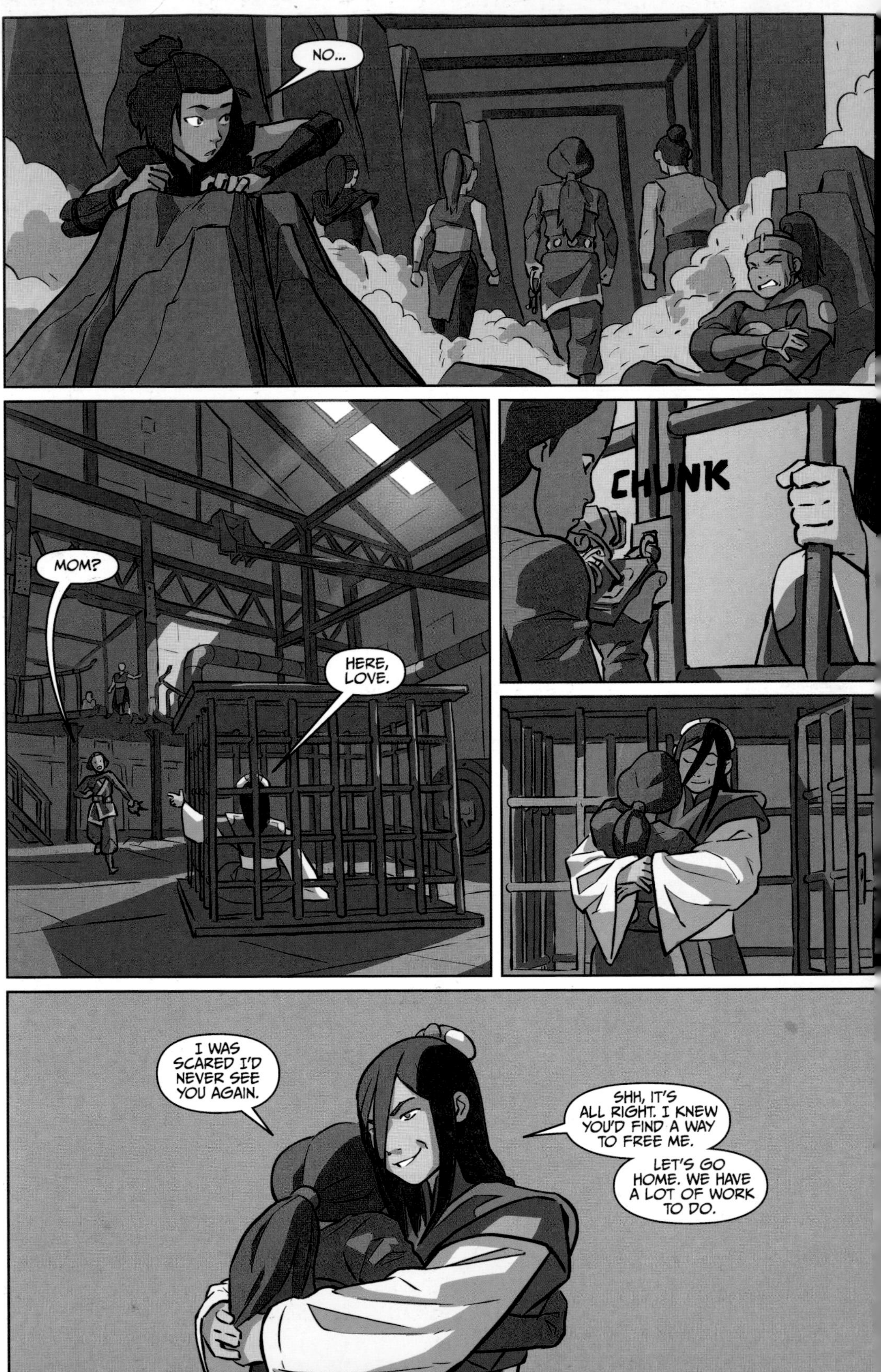
NO...
MOM?
HERE, LOVE.
CHUNK
I WAS SCARED I'D NEVER SEE YOU AGAIN.
SHH, IT'S ALL RIGHT. I KNEW YOU'D FIND A WAY TO FREE ME.
LET'S GO HOME. WE HAVE A LOT OF WORK TO DO.

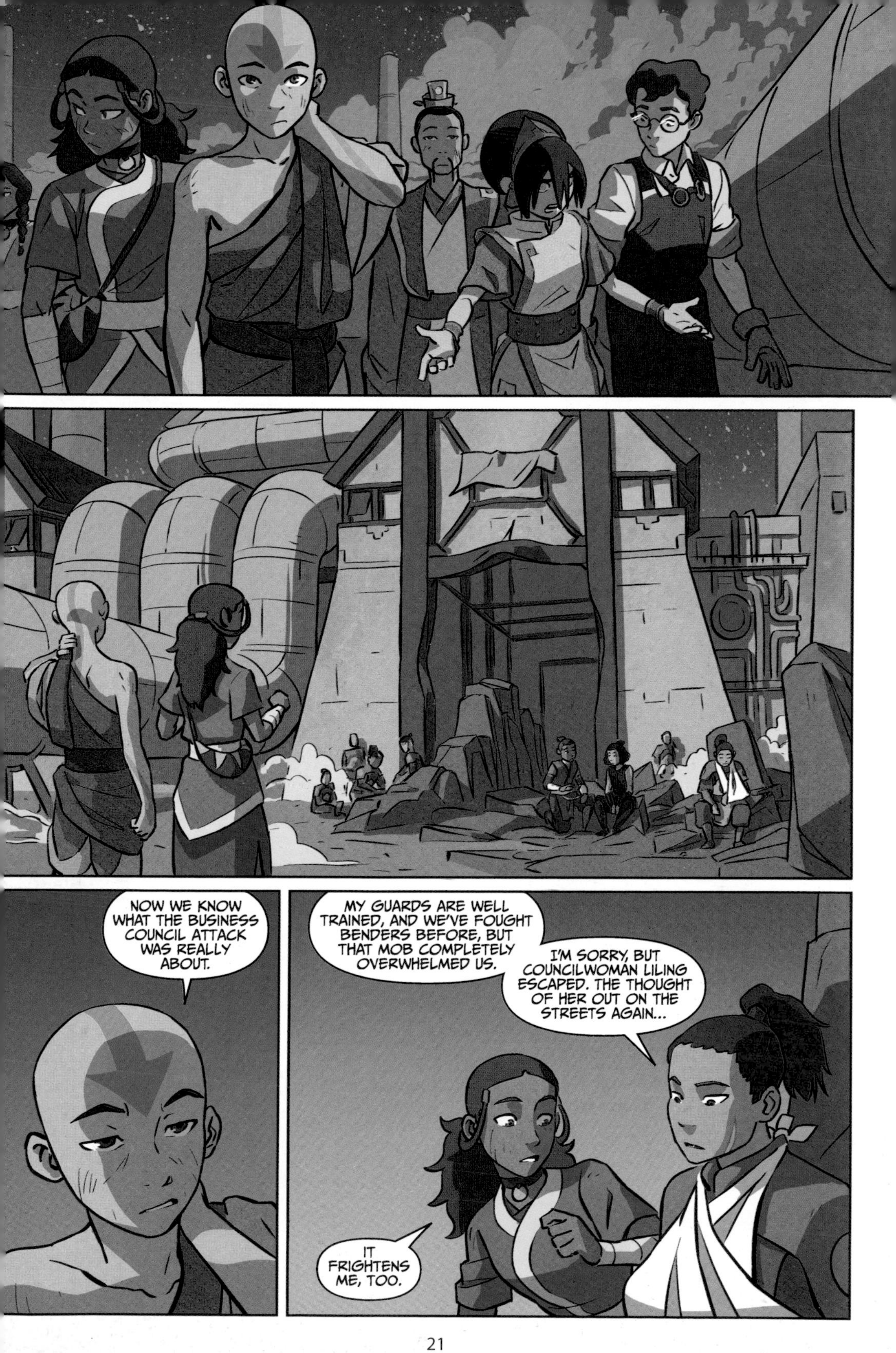
NOW WE KNOW WHAT THE BUSINESS COUNCIL ATTACK WAS REALLY ABOUT.
MY GUARDS ARE WELL TRAINED, AND WE'VE FOUGHT BENDERS BEFORE, BUT THAT MOB COMPLETELY OVERWHELMED US.
I'M SORRY, BUT COUNCILWOMAN LILING ESCAPED. THE THOUGHT OF HER OUT ON THE STREETS AGAIN...
IT FRIGHTENS ME, TOO.

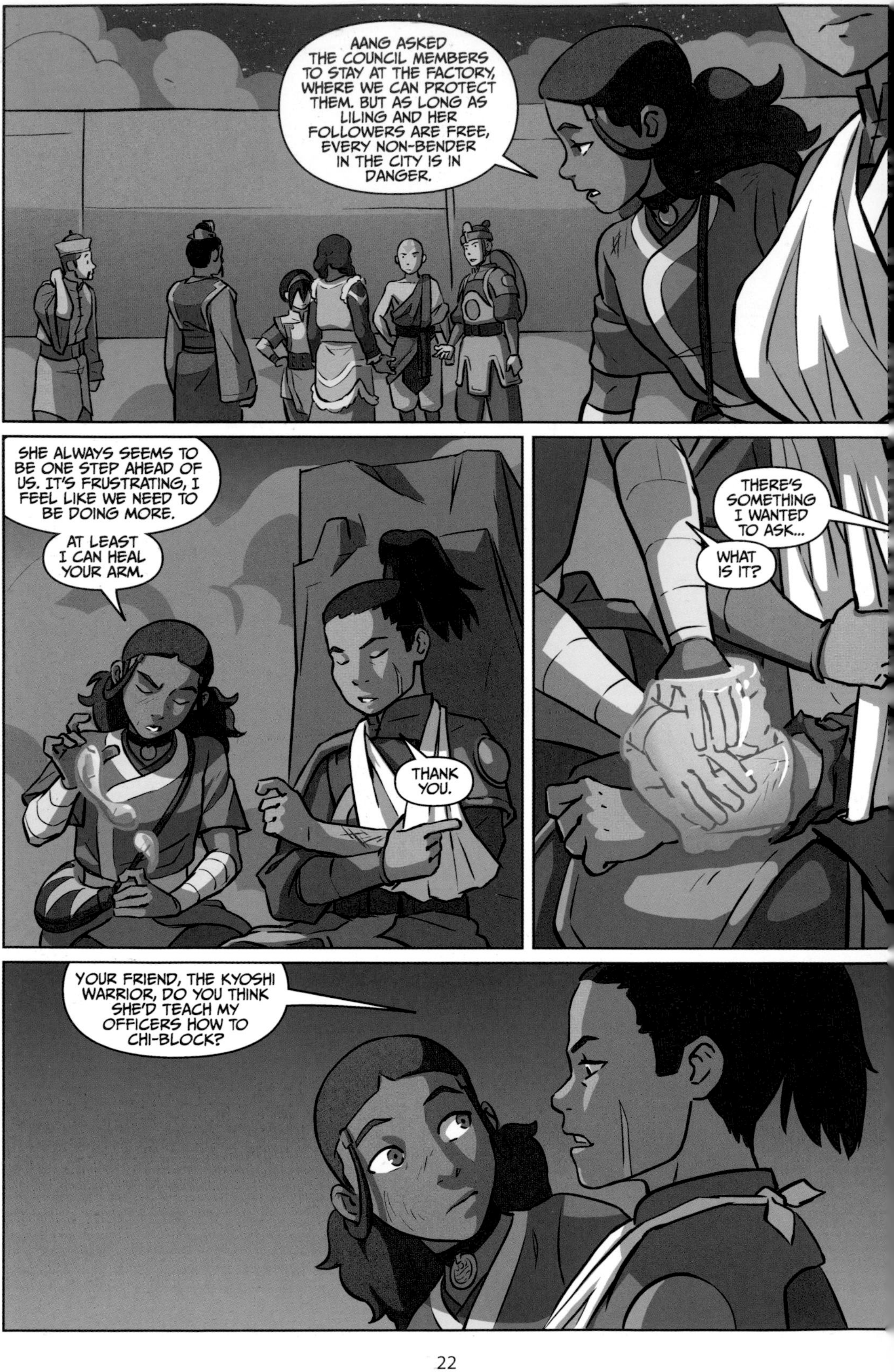
AANG ASKED THE COUNCIL MEMBERS TO STAY AT THE FACTORY, WHERE WE CAN PROTECT THEM. BUT AS LONG AS LILING AND HER FOLLOWERS ARE FREE, EVERY NON-BENDER IN THE CITY IS IN DANGER.
SHE ALWAYS SEEMS TO BE ONE STEP AHEAD OF US. IT'S FRUSTRATING, I FEEL LIKE WE NEED TO BE DOING MORE.
AT LEAST I CAN HEAL YOUR ARM.
THANK YOU.
THERE'S SOMETHING I WANTED TO ASK...
WHAT IS IT?
YOUR FRIEND, THE KYOSHI WARRIOR, DO YOU THINK SHE'D TEACH MY OFFICERS HOW TO CHI-BLOCK?

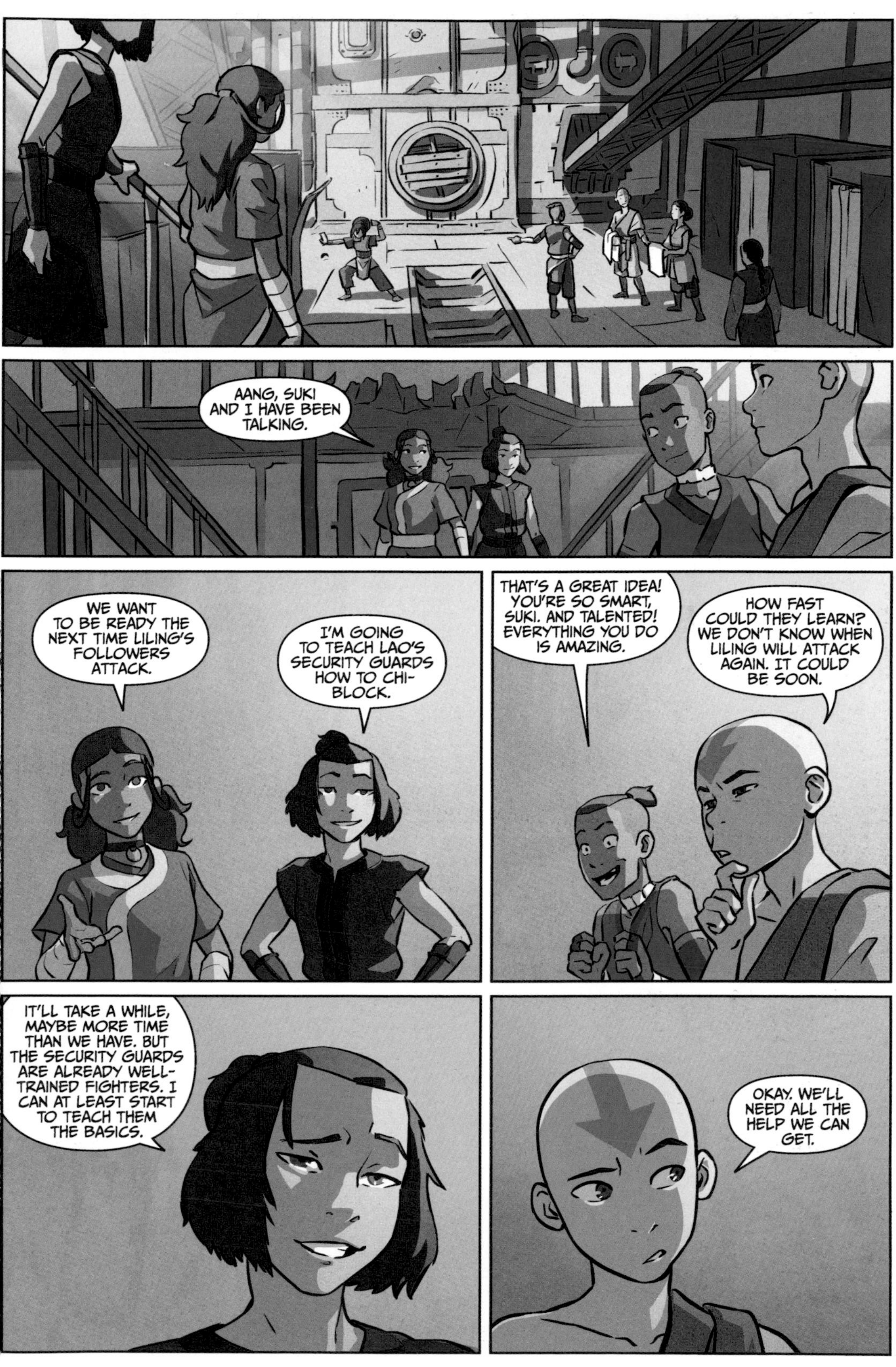
AANG, SUKI AND I HAVE BEEN TALKING.
WE WANT TO BE READY THE NEXT TIME LILING'S FOLLOWERS ATTACK.
I'M GOING TO TEACH LAO'S SECURITY GUARDS HOW TO CHI-BLOCK.
THAT'S A GREAT IDEA! YOU'RE SO SMART, SUKI. AND TALENTED! EVERYTHING YOU DO IS AMAZING.
HOW FAST COULD THEY LEARN? WE DON'T KNOW WHEN LILING WILL ATTACK AGAIN. IT COULD BE SOON.
IT'LL TAKE A WHILE, MAYBE MORE TIME THAN WE HAVE. BUT THE SECURITY GUARDS ARE ALREADY WELL-TRAINED FIGHTERS. I CAN AT LEAST START TO TEACH THEM THE BASICS.
OKAY. WE'LL NEED ALL THE HELP WE CAN GET.

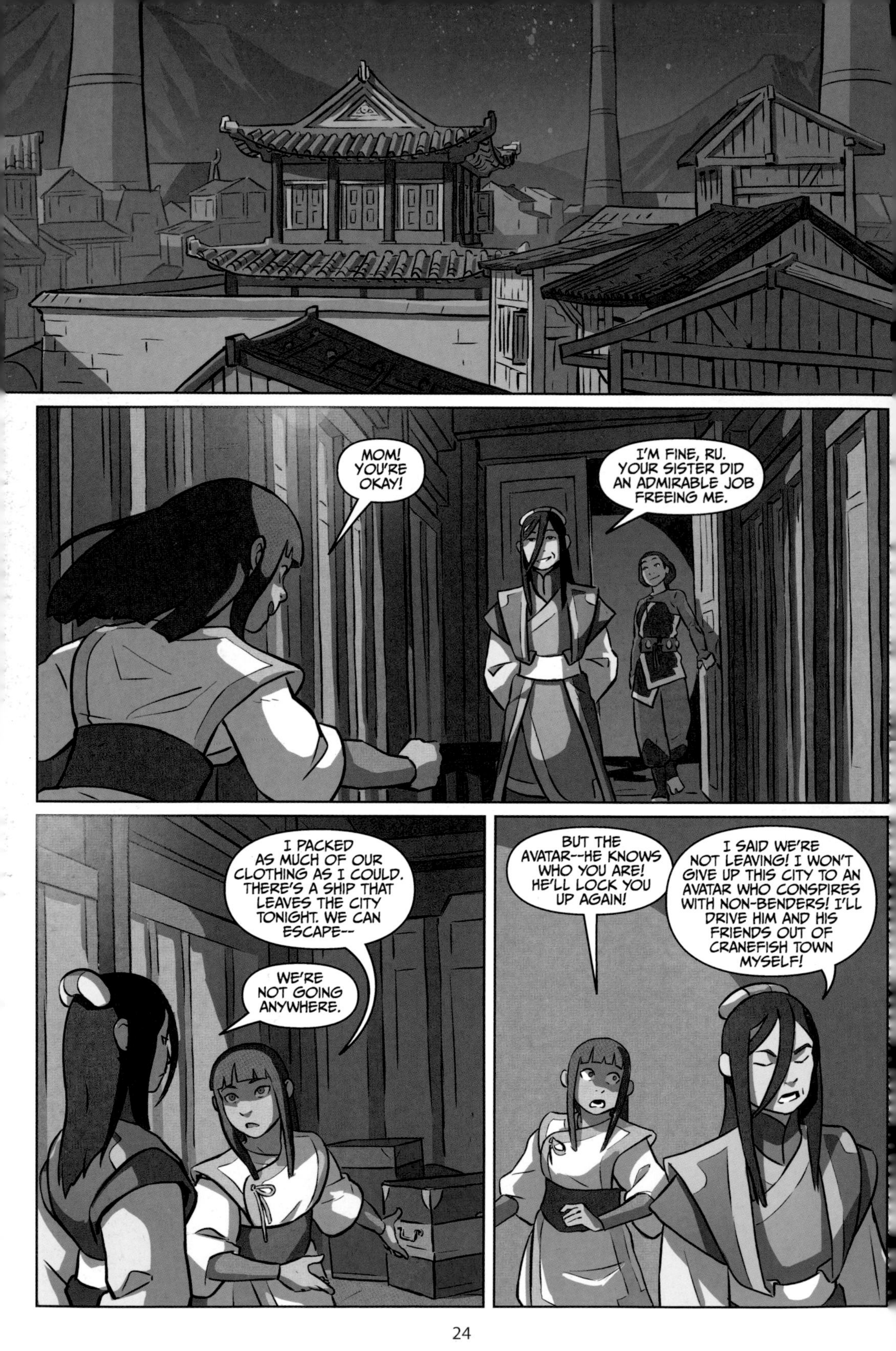
MOM! YOU'RE OKAY!
I'M FINE, RU. YOUR SISTER DID AN ADMIRABLE JOB FREEING ME.
I PACKED AS MUCH OF OUR CLOTHING AS I COULD. THERE'S A SHIP THAT LEAVES THE CITY TONIGHT. WE CAN ESCAPE--
WE'RE NOT GOING ANYWHERE.
BUT THE AVATAR--HE KNOWS WHO YOU ARE! HE'LL LOCK YOU UP AGAIN!
I SAID WE'RE NOT LEAVING! I WON'T GIVE UP THIS CITY TO AN AVATAR WHO CONSPIRES WITH NON-BENDERS! I'LL DRIVE HIM AND HIS FRIENDS OUT OF CRANEFISH TOWN MYSELF!

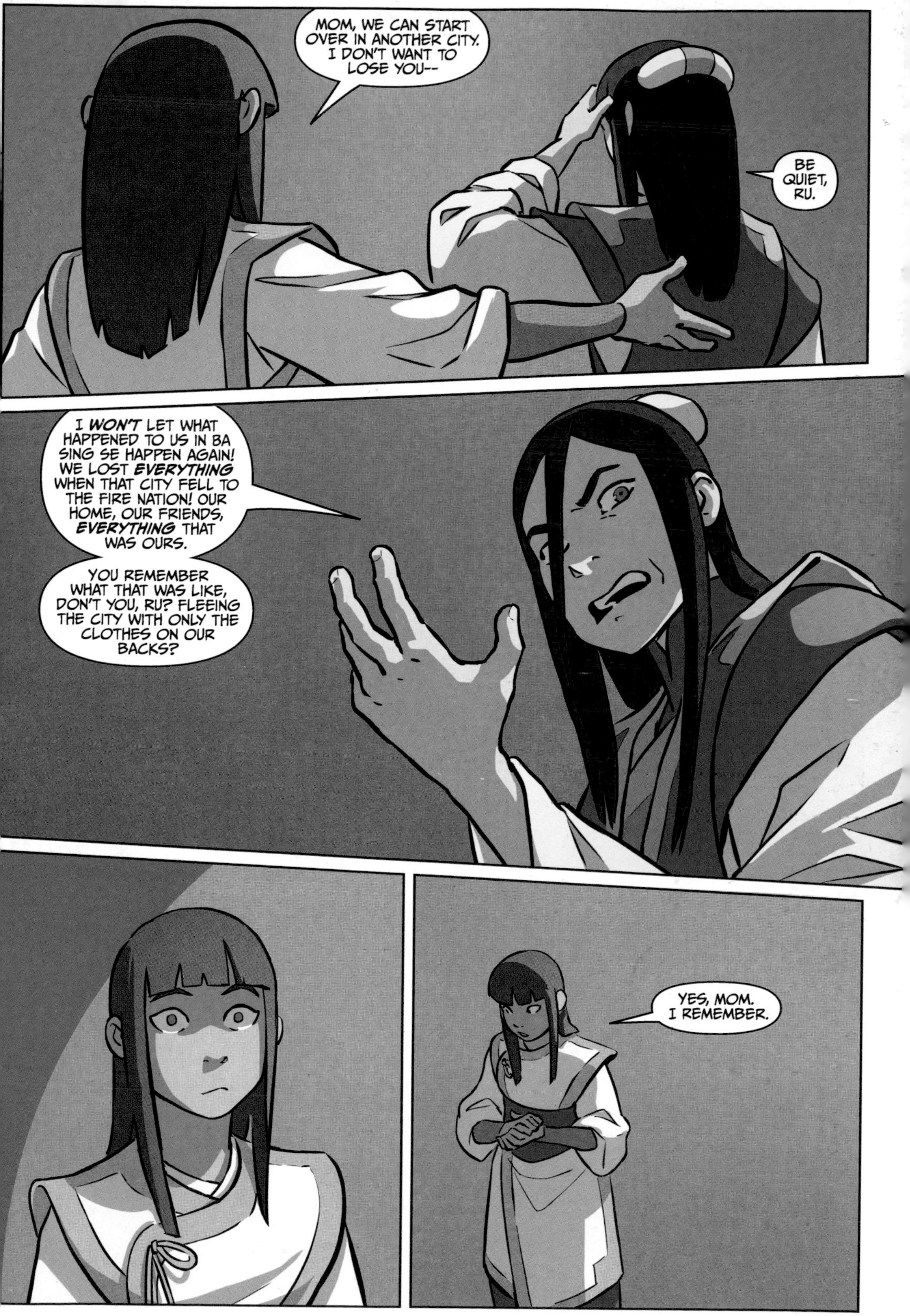
MOM, WE CAN START OVER IN ANOTHER CITY. I DON'T WANT TO LOSE YOU--
BE QUIET, RU.
I *WON'T* LET WHAT HAPPENED TO US IN BA SING SE HAPPEN AGAIN! WE LOST *EVERYTHING* WHEN THAT CITY FELL TO THE FIRE NATION! OUR HOME, OUR FRIENDS, *EVERYTHING* THAT WAS OURS.
YOU REMEMBER WHAT THAT WAS LIKE, DON'T YOU, RU? FLEEING THE CITY WITH ONLY THE CLOTHES ON OUR BACKS?
YES, MOM. I REMEMBER.

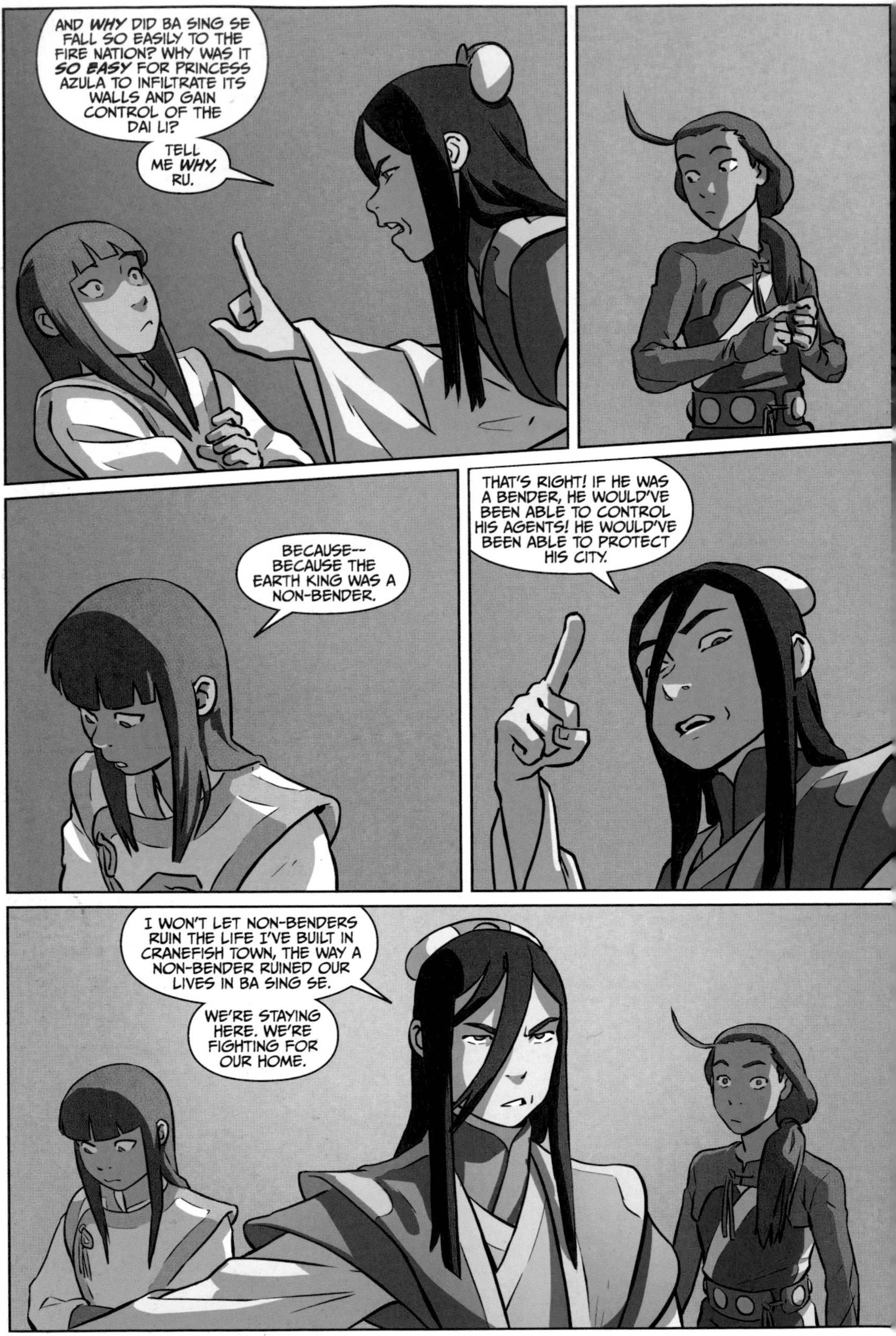
AND WHY DID BA SING SE FALL SO EASILY TO THE FIRE NATION? WHY WAS IT SO EASY FOR PRINCESS AZULA TO INFILTRATE ITS WALLS AND GAIN CONTROL OF THE DAI LI?
TELL ME WHY, RU.
BECAUSE-- BECAUSE THE EARTH KING WAS A NON-BENDER.
THAT'S RIGHT! IF HE WAS A BENDER, HE WOULD'VE BEEN ABLE TO CONTROL HIS AGENTS! HE WOULD'VE BEEN ABLE TO PROTECT HIS CITY.
I WON'T LET NON-BENDERS RUIN THE LIFE I'VE BUILT IN CRANEFISH TOWN, THE WAY A NON-BENDER RUINED OUR LIVES IN BA SING SE.
WE'RE STAYING HERE. WE'RE FIGHTING FOR OUR HOME.

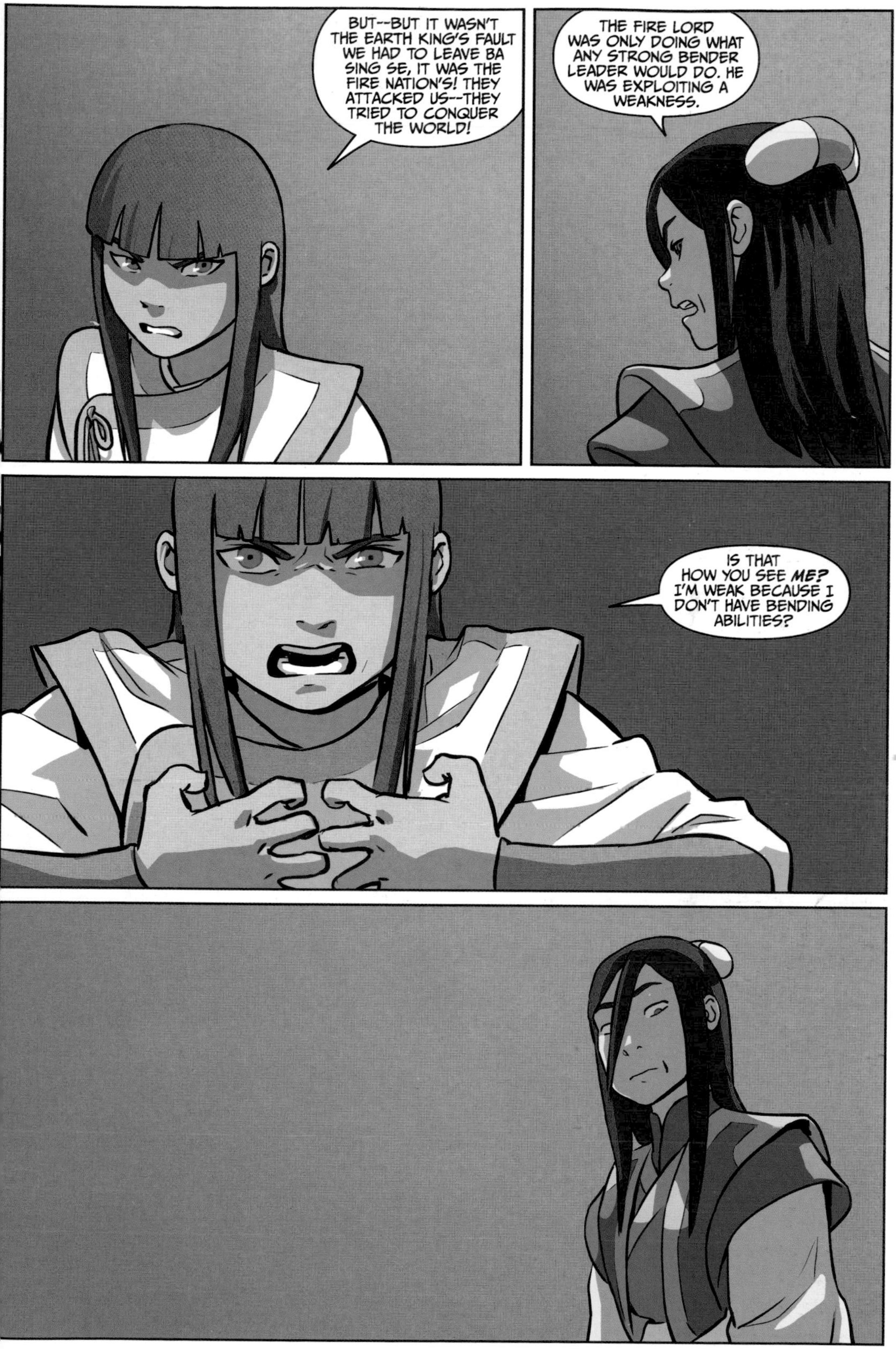
BUT--BUT IT WASN'T THE EARTH KING'S FAULT WE HAD TO LEAVE BA SING SE, IT WAS THE FIRE NATION'S! THEY ATTACKED US--THEY TRIED TO CONQUER THE WORLD!
THE FIRE LORD WAS ONLY DOING WHAT ANY STRONG BENDER LEADER WOULD DO. HE WAS EXPLOITING A WEAKNESS.
IS THAT HOW YOU SEE *ME?* I'M WEAK BECAUSE I DON'T HAVE BENDING ABILITIES?

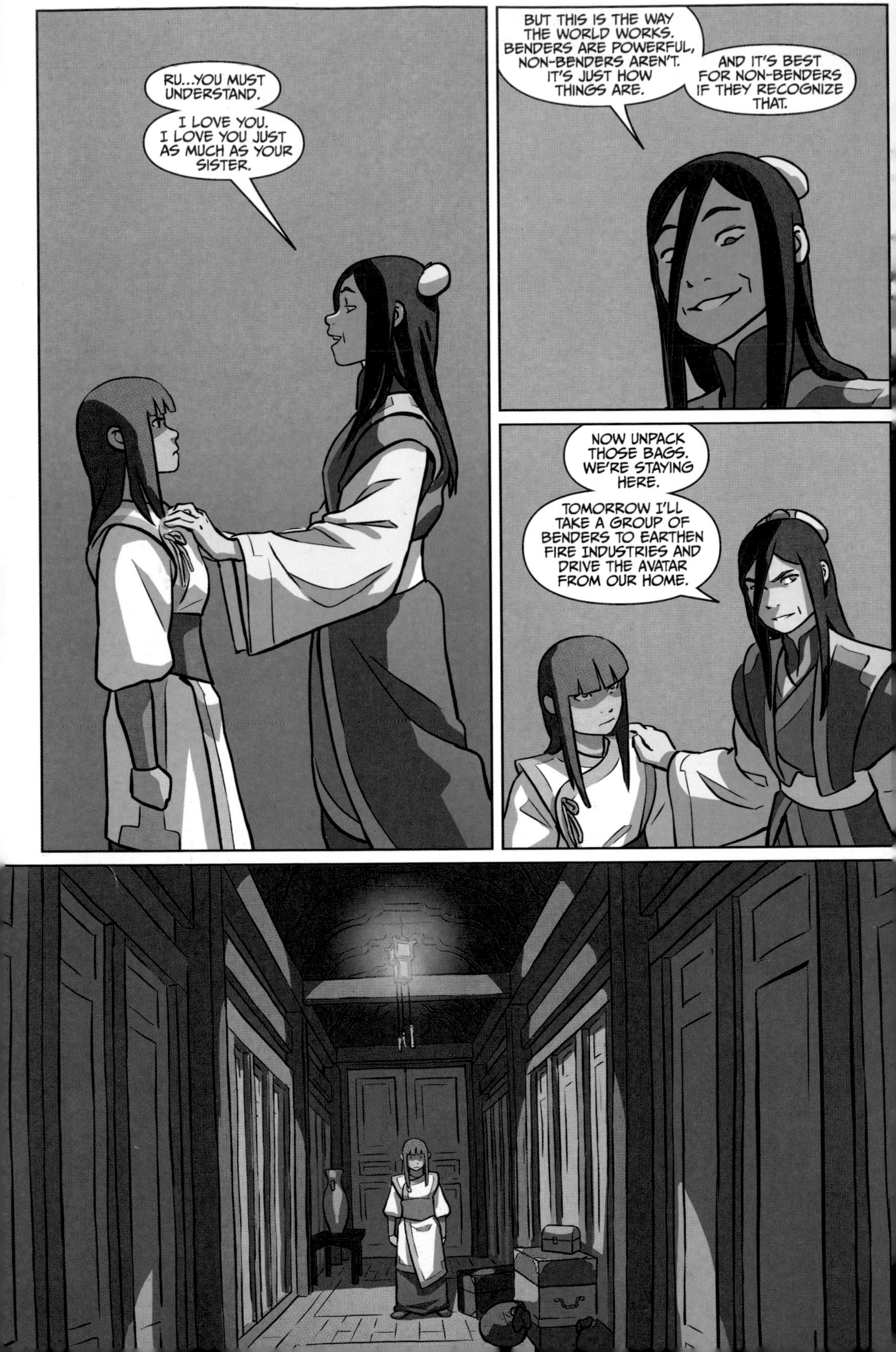
RU...YOU MUST UNDERSTAND.
I LOVE YOU. I LOVE YOU JUST AS MUCH AS YOUR SISTER.
BUT THIS IS THE WAY THE WORLD WORKS. BENDERS ARE POWERFUL, NON-BENDERS AREN'T. IT'S JUST HOW THINGS ARE.
AND IT'S BEST FOR NON-BENDERS IF THEY RECOGNIZE THAT.
NOW UNPACK THOSE BAGS. WE'RE STAYING HERE.
TOMORROW I'LL TAKE A GROUP OF BENDERS TO EARTHEN FIRE INDUSTRIES AND DRIVE THE AVATAR FROM OUR HOME.

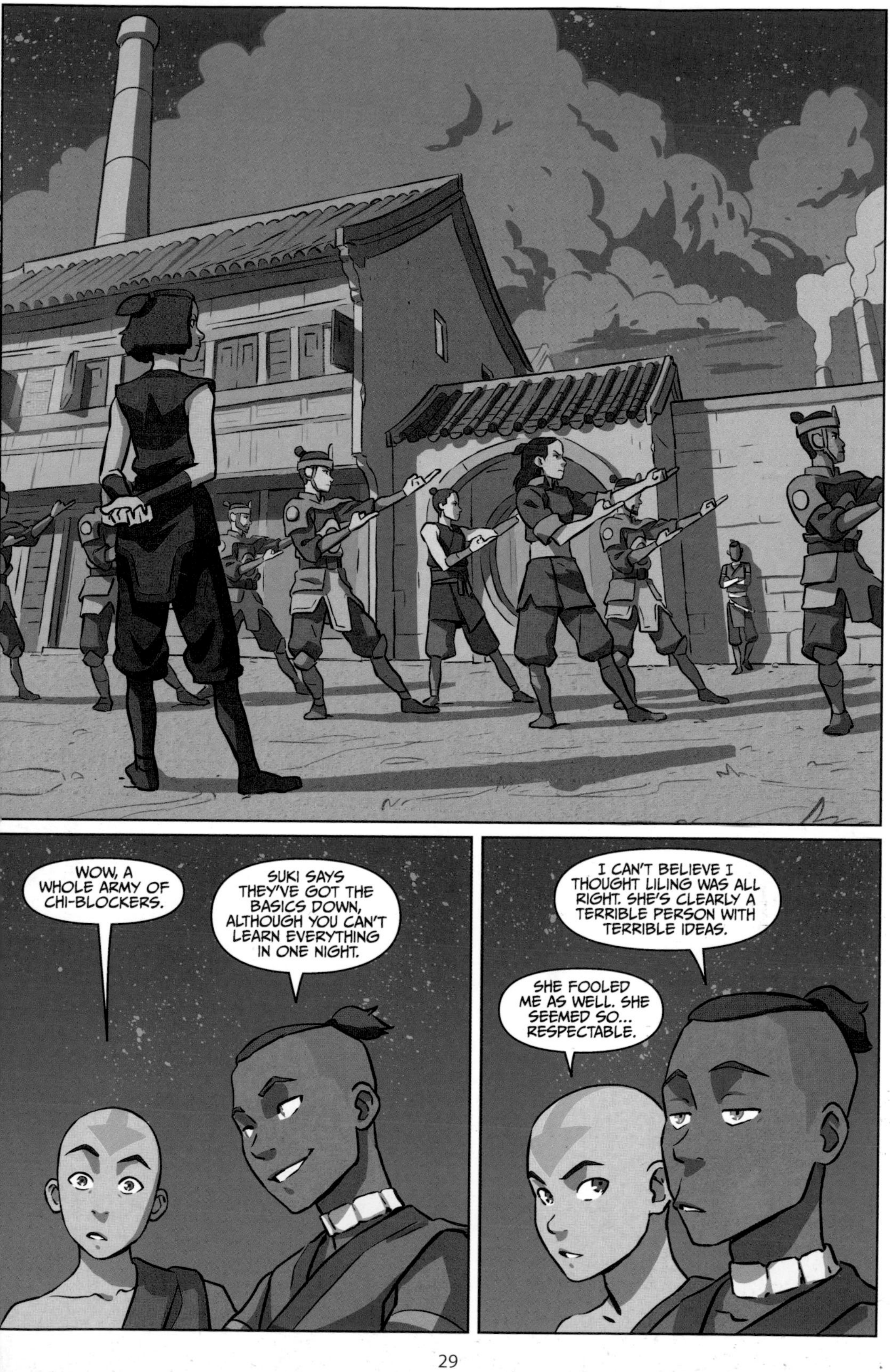
WOW, A WHOLE ARMY OF CHI-BLOCKERS.
SUKI SAYS THEY'VE GOT THE BASICS DOWN, ALTHOUGH YOU CAN'T LEARN EVERYTHING IN ONE NIGHT.
I CAN'T BELIEVE I THOUGHT LILING WAS ALL RIGHT. SHE'S CLEARLY A TERRIBLE PERSON WITH TERRIBLE IDEAS.
SHE FOOLED ME AS WELL. SHE SEEMED SO... RESPECTABLE.

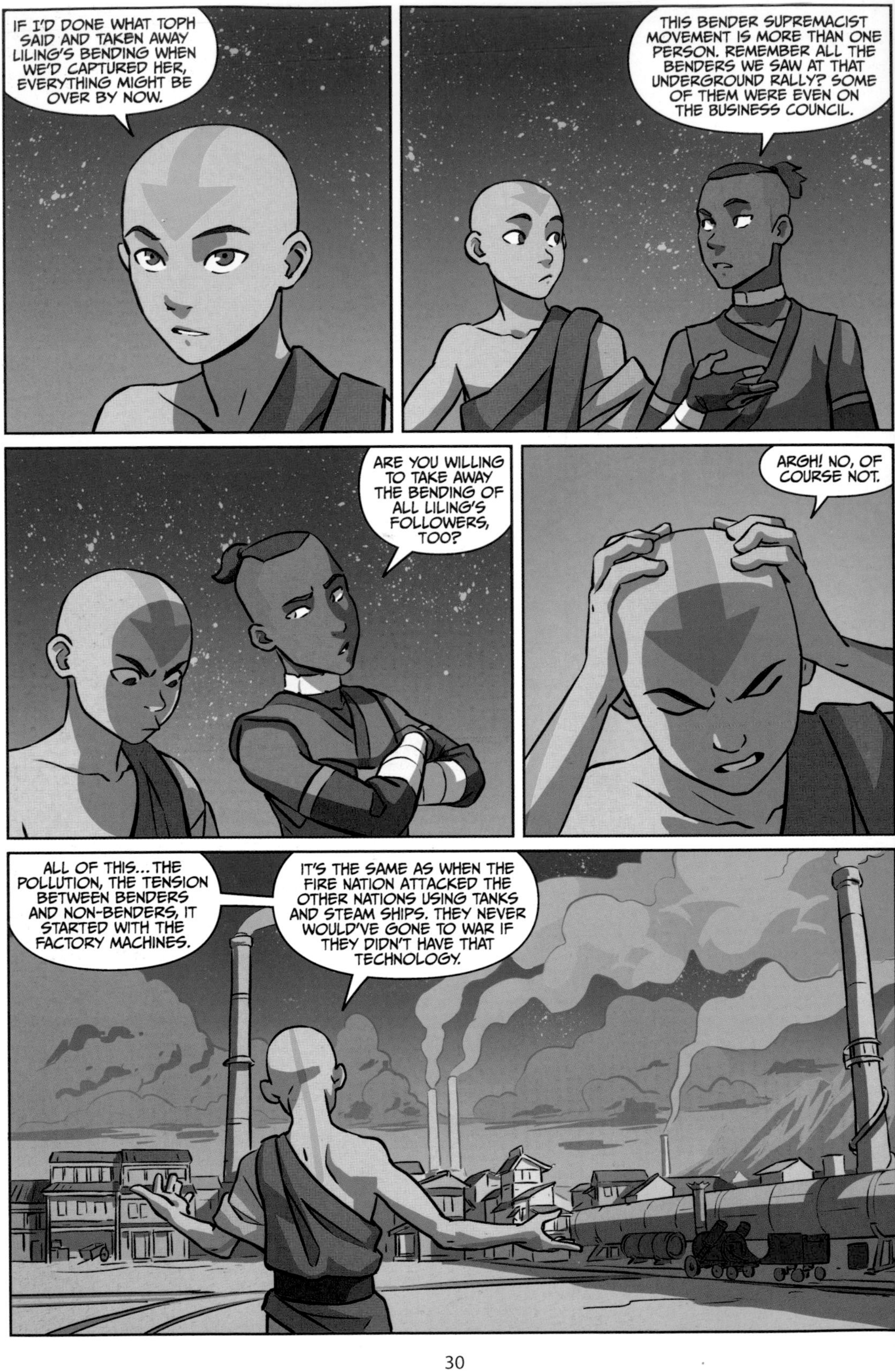
IF I'D DONE WHAT TOPH SAID AND TAKEN AWAY LILING'S BENDING WHEN WE'D CAPTURED HER, EVERYTHING MIGHT BE OVER BY NOW.
THIS BENDER SUPREMACIST MOVEMENT IS MORE THAN ONE PERSON. REMEMBER ALL THE BENDERS WE SAW AT THAT UNDERGROUND RALLY? SOME OF THEM WERE EVEN ON THE BUSINESS COUNCIL.
ARE YOU WILLING TO TAKE AWAY THE BENDING OF ALL LILING'S FOLLOWERS, TOO?
ARGH! NO, OF COURSE NOT.
ALL OF THIS...THE POLLUTION, THE TENSION BETWEEN BENDERS AND NON-BENDERS, IT STARTED WITH THE FACTORY MACHINES.
IT'S THE SAME AS WHEN THE FIRE NATION ATTACKED THE OTHER NATIONS USING TANKS AND STEAM SHIPS. THEY NEVER WOULD'VE GONE TO WAR IF THEY DIDN'T HAVE THAT TECHNOLOGY.

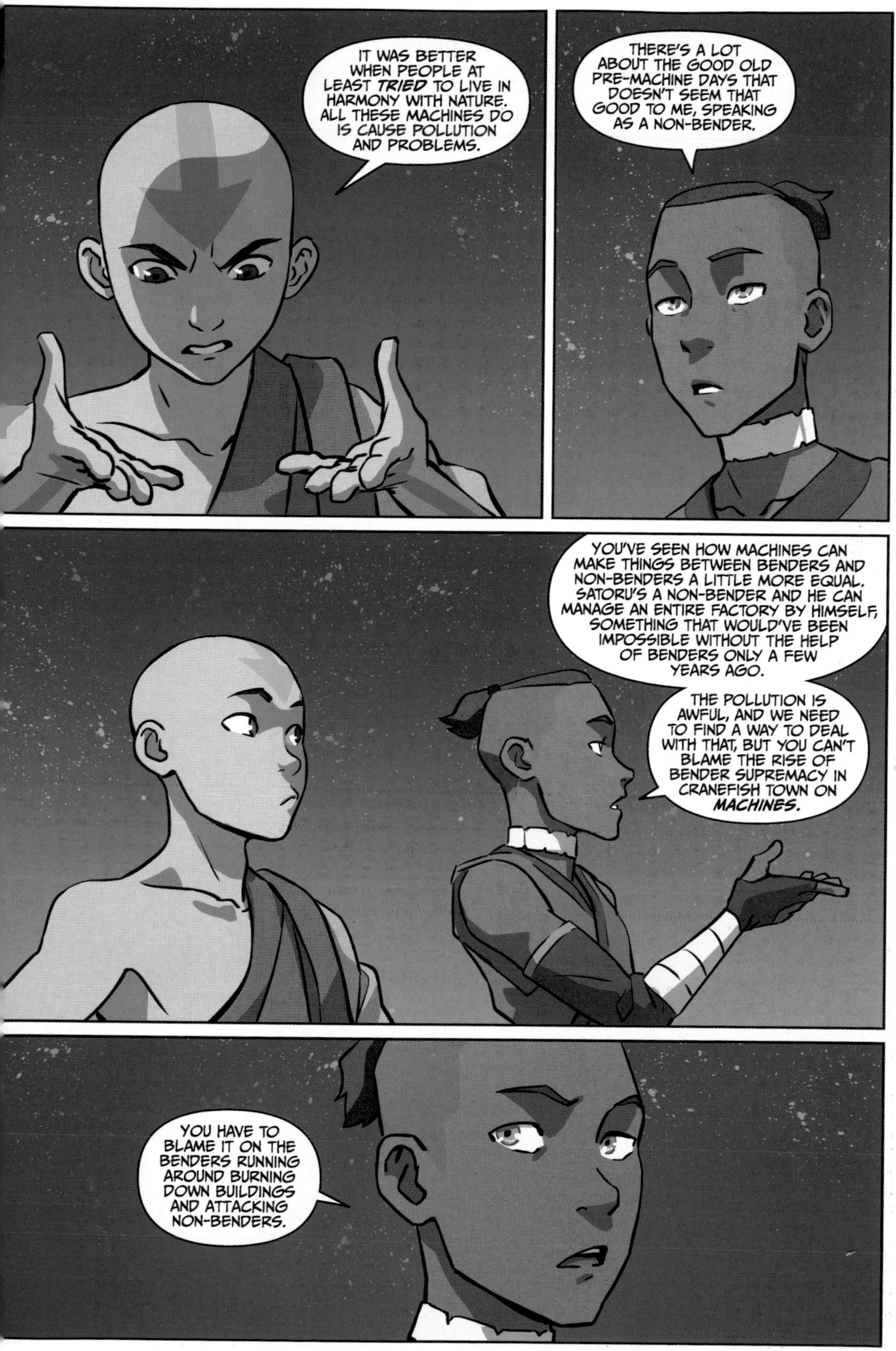
IT WAS BETTER WHEN PEOPLE AT LEAST TRIED TO LIVE IN HARMONY WITH NATURE. ALL THESE MACHINES DO IS CAUSE POLLUTION AND PROBLEMS.
THERE'S A LOT ABOUT THE GOOD OLD PRE-MACHINE DAYS THAT DOESN'T SEEM THAT GOOD TO ME, SPEAKING AS A NON-BENDER.
YOU'VE SEEN HOW MACHINES CAN MAKE THINGS BETWEEN BENDERS AND NON-BENDERS A LITTLE MORE EQUAL. SATORU'S A NON-BENDER AND HE CAN MANAGE AN ENTIRE FACTORY BY HIMSELF, SOMETHING THAT WOULD'VE BEEN IMPOSSIBLE WITHOUT THE HELP OF BENDERS ONLY A FEW YEARS AGO.
THE POLLUTION IS AWFUL, AND WE NEED TO FIND A WAY TO DEAL WITH THAT, BUT YOU CAN'T BLAME THE RISE OF BENDER SUPREMACY IN CRANEFISH TOWN ON MACHINES.
YOU HAVE TO BLAME IT ON THE BENDERS RUNNING AROUND BURNING DOWN BUILDINGS AND ATTACKING NON-BENDERS.

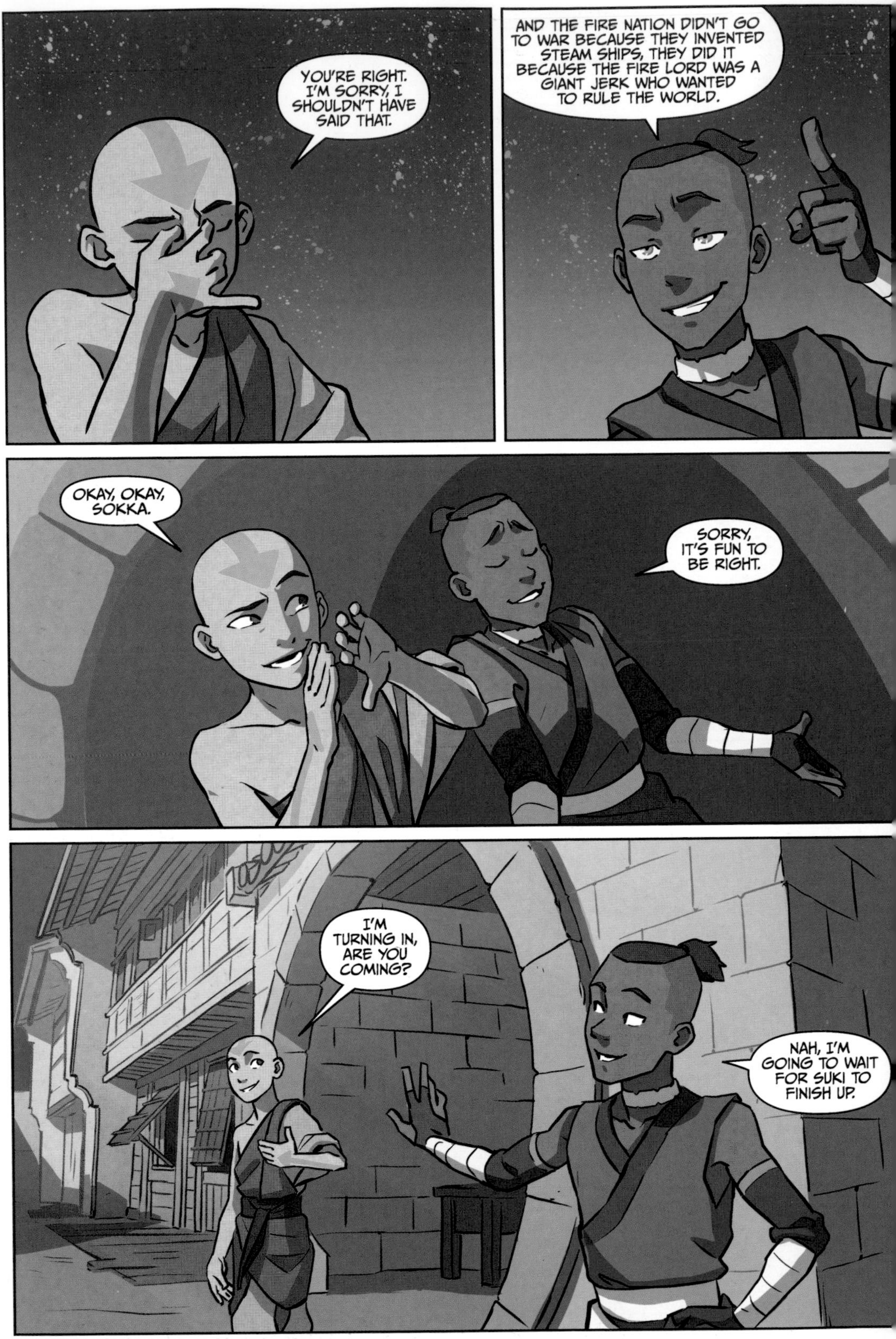
YOU'RE RIGHT. I'M SORRY, I SHOULDN'T HAVE SAID THAT.
AND THE FIRE NATION DIDN'T GO TO WAR BECAUSE THEY INVENTED STEAM SHIPS, THEY DID IT BECAUSE THE FIRE LORD WAS A GIANT JERK WHO WANTED TO RULE THE WORLD.
OKAY, OKAY, SOKKA.
SORRY, IT'S FUN TO BE RIGHT.
I'M TURNING IN, ARE YOU COMING?
NAH, I'M GOING TO WAIT FOR SUKI TO FINISH UP.

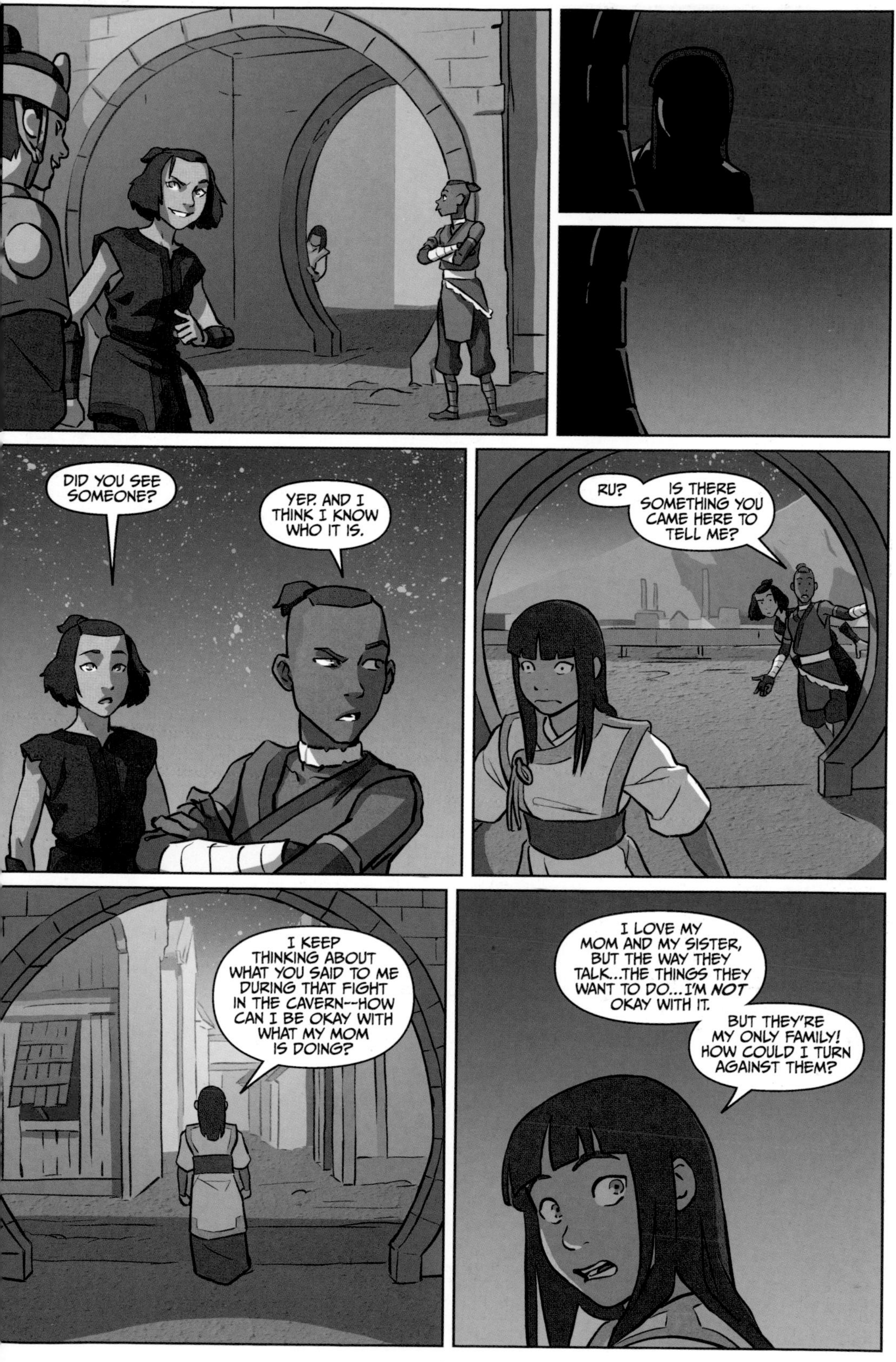
DID YOU SEE SOMEONE?
YEP. AND I THINK I KNOW WHO IT IS.
RU?
IS THERE SOMETHING YOU CAME HERE TO TELL ME?
I KEEP THINKING ABOUT WHAT YOU SAID TO ME DURING THAT FIGHT IN THE CAVERN--HOW CAN I BE OKAY WITH WHAT MY MOM IS DOING?
I LOVE MY MOM AND MY SISTER, BUT THE WAY THEY TALK...THE THINGS THEY WANT TO DO...I'M NOT OKAY WITH IT.
BUT THEY'RE MY ONLY FAMILY! HOW COULD I TURN AGAINST THEM?

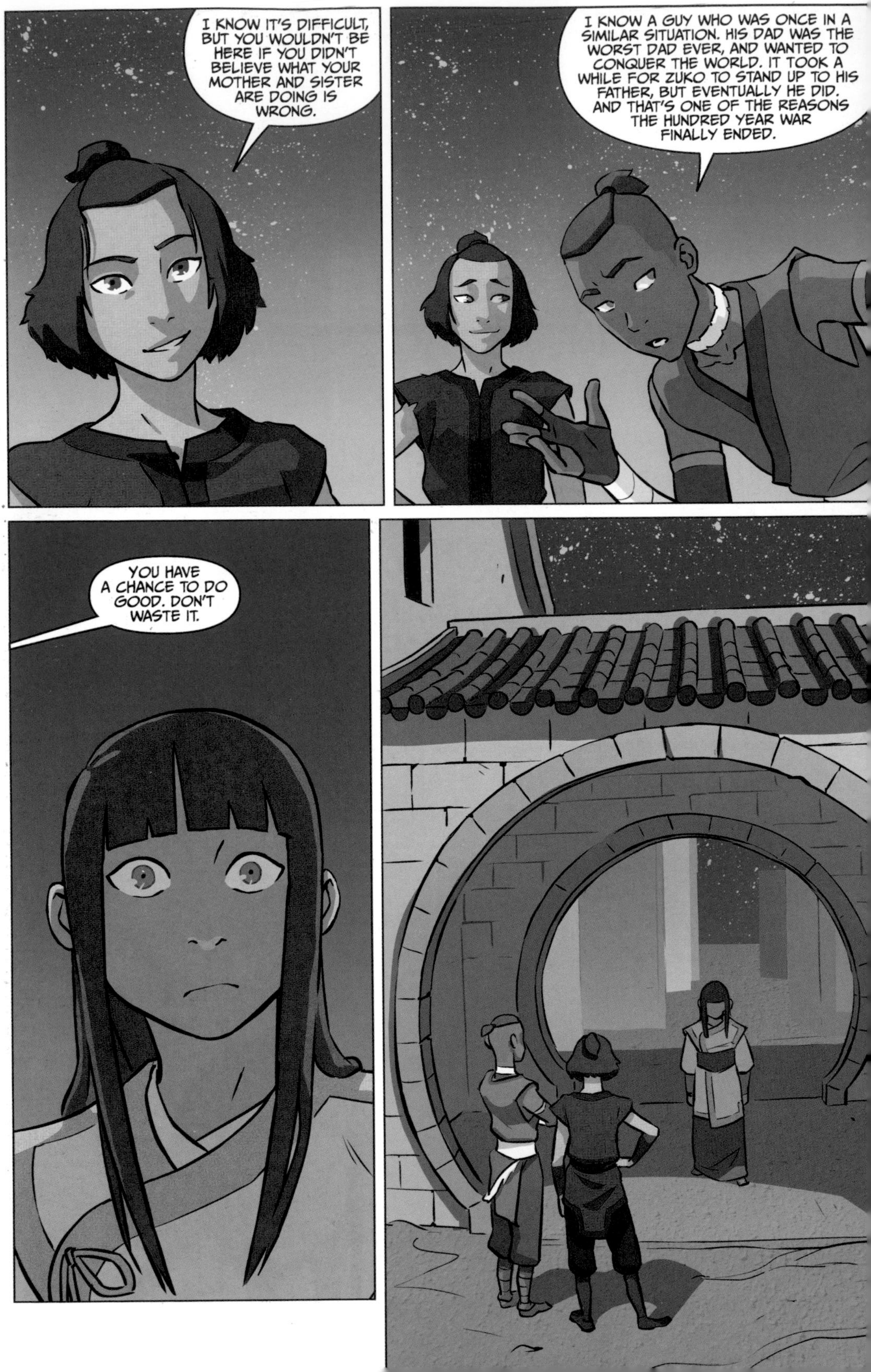
I KNOW IT'S DIFFICULT, BUT YOU WOULDN'T BE HERE IF YOU DIDN'T BELIEVE WHAT YOUR MOTHER AND SISTER ARE DOING IS WRONG.
I KNOW A GUY WHO WAS ONCE IN A SIMILAR SITUATION. HIS DAD WAS THE WORST DAD EVER, AND WANTED TO CONQUER THE WORLD. IT TOOK A WHILE FOR ZUKO TO STAND UP TO HIS FATHER, BUT EVENTUALLY HE DID. AND THAT'S ONE OF THE REASONS THE HUNDRED YEAR WAR FINALLY ENDED.
YOU HAVE A CHANCE TO DO GOOD. DON'T WASTE IT.

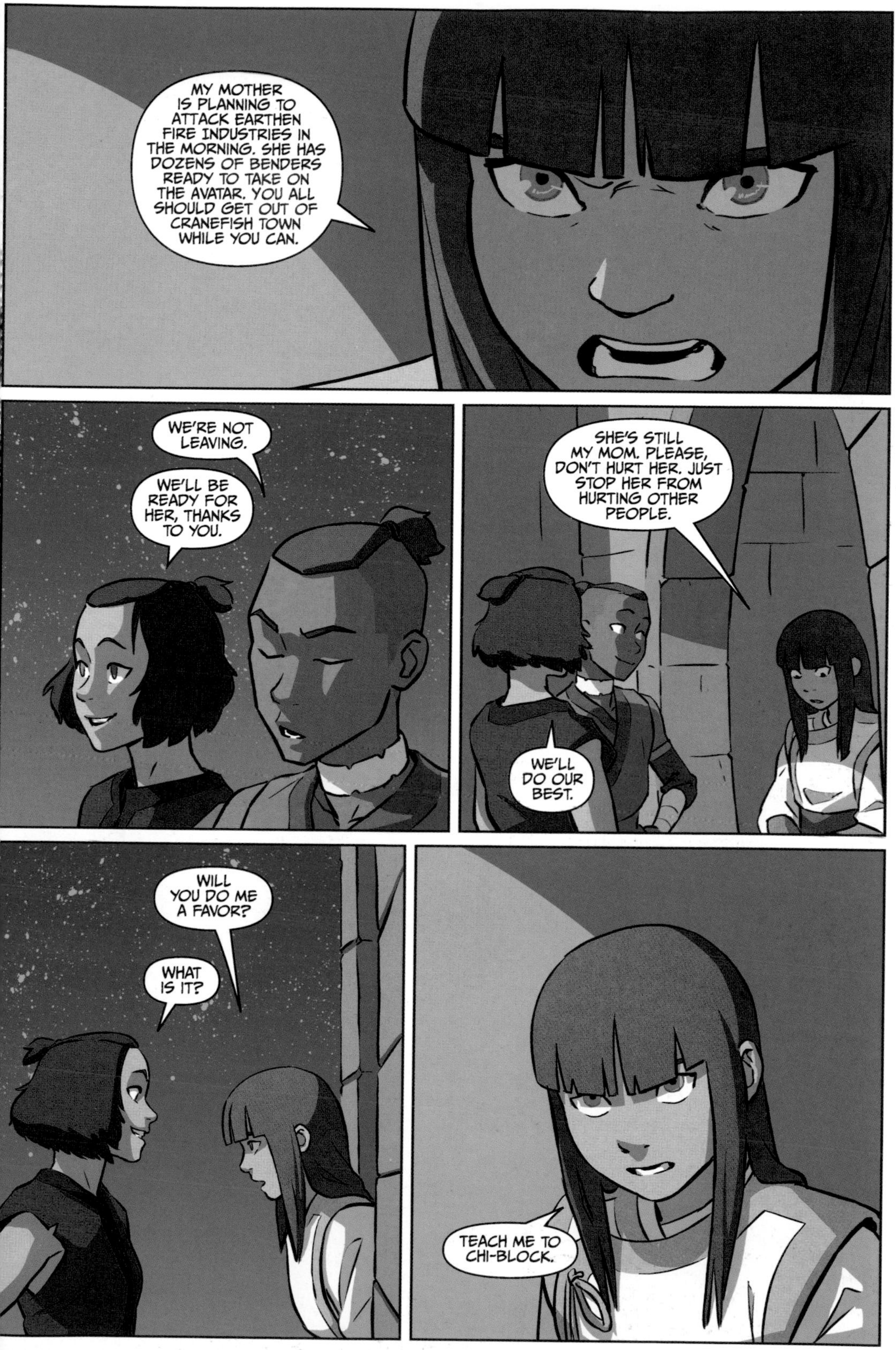
MY MOTHER IS PLANNING TO ATTACK EARTHEN FIRE INDUSTRIES IN THE MORNING. SHE HAS DOZENS OF BENDERS READY TO TAKE ON THE AVATAR. YOU ALL SHOULD GET OUT OF CRANEFISH TOWN WHILE YOU CAN.
WE'RE NOT LEAVING.
WE'LL BE READY FOR HER, THANKS TO YOU.
SHE'S STILL MY MOM. PLEASE, DON'T HURT HER. JUST STOP HER FROM HURTING OTHER PEOPLE.
WE'LL DO OUR BEST.
WILL YOU DO ME A FAVOR?
WHAT IS IT?
TEACH ME TO CHI-BLOCK.

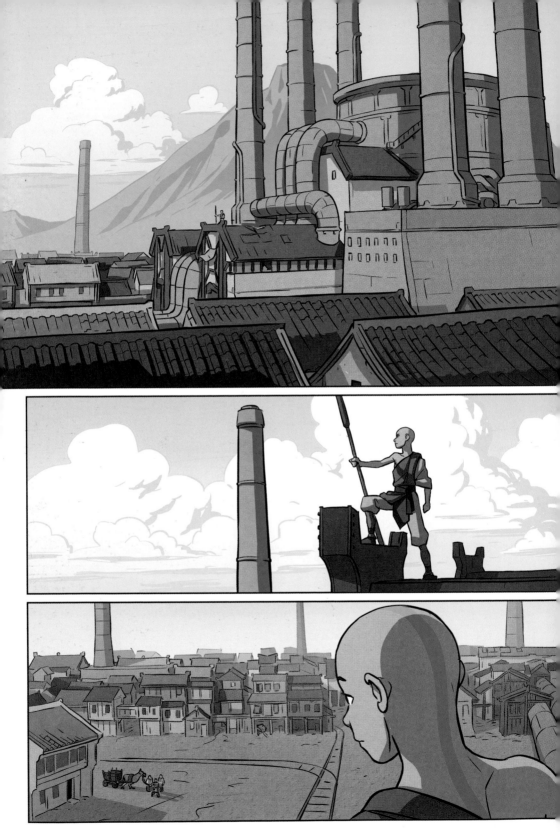

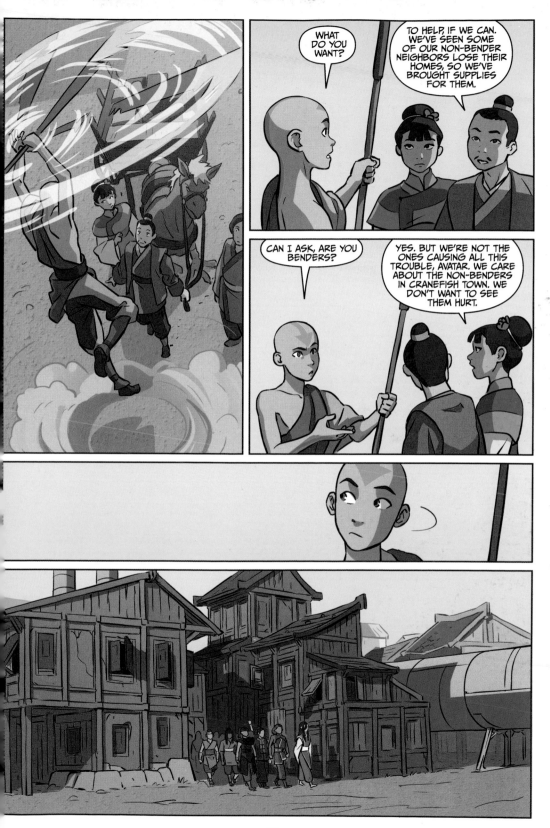

WHAT DO YOU WANT?

TO HELP, IF WE CAN. WE'VE SEEN SOME OF OUR NON-BENDER NEIGHBORS LOSE THEIR HOMES, SO WE'VE BROUGHT SUPPLIES FOR THEM.

CAN I ASK, ARE YOU BENDERS?

YES. BUT WE'RE NOT THE ONES CAUSING ALL THIS TROUBLE, AVATAR. WE CARE ABOUT THE NON-BENDERS IN CRANEFISH TOWN. WE DON'T WANT TO SEE THEM HURT.

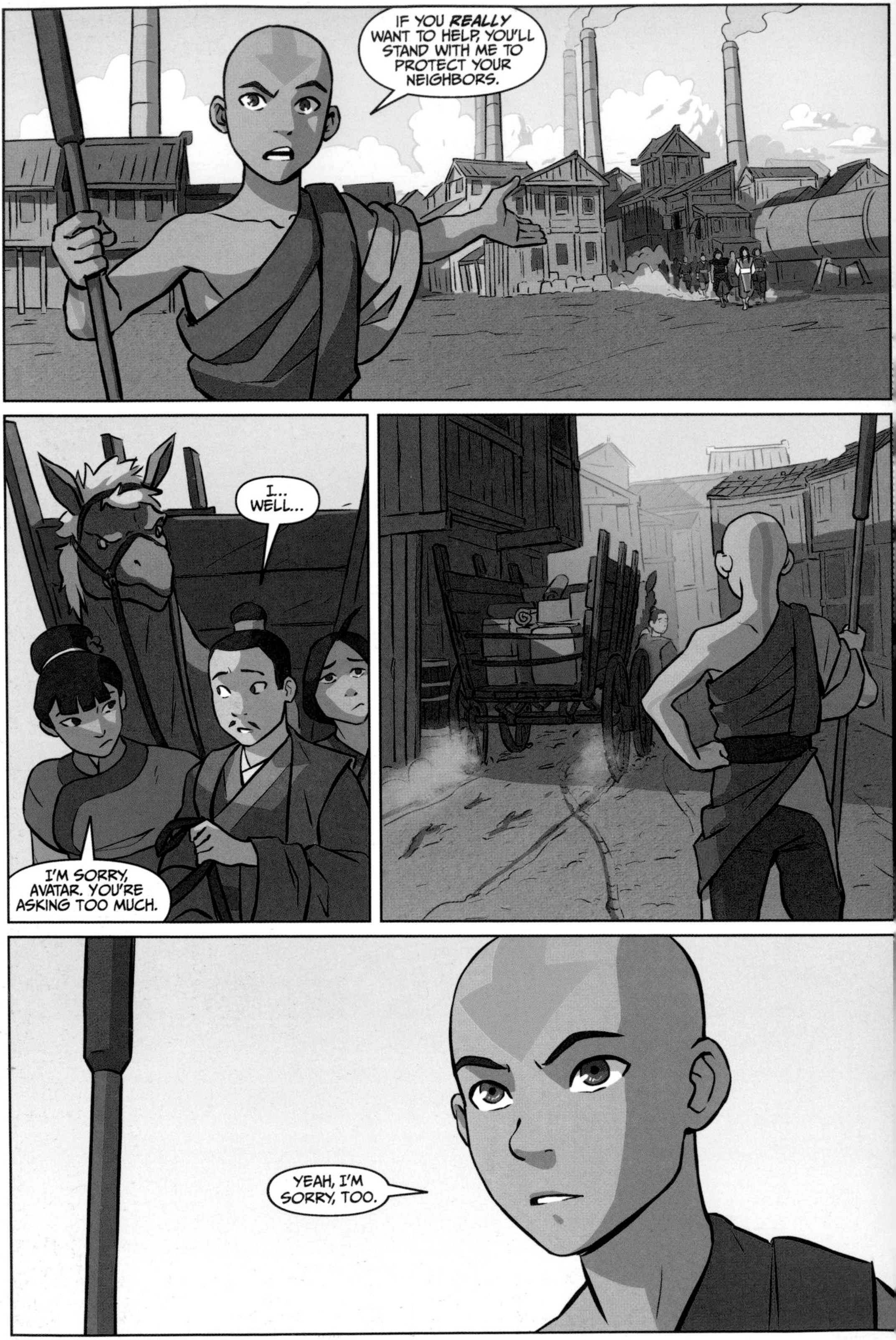
IF YOU REALLY WANT TO HELP, YOU'LL STAND WITH ME TO PROTECT YOUR NEIGHBORS.
I... WELL...
I'M SORRY, AVATAR. YOU'RE ASKING TOO MUCH.
YEAH, I'M SORRY, TOO.

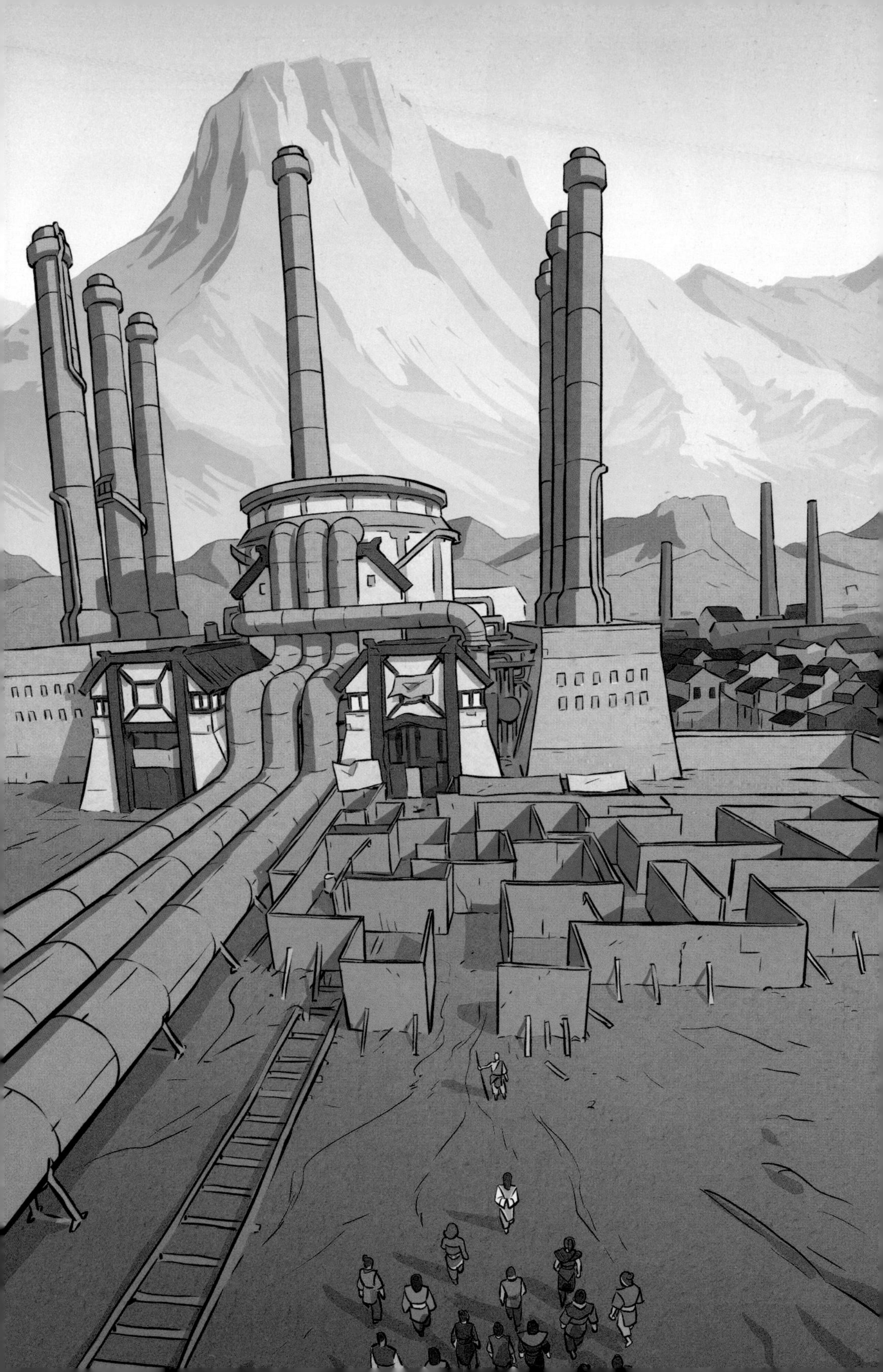

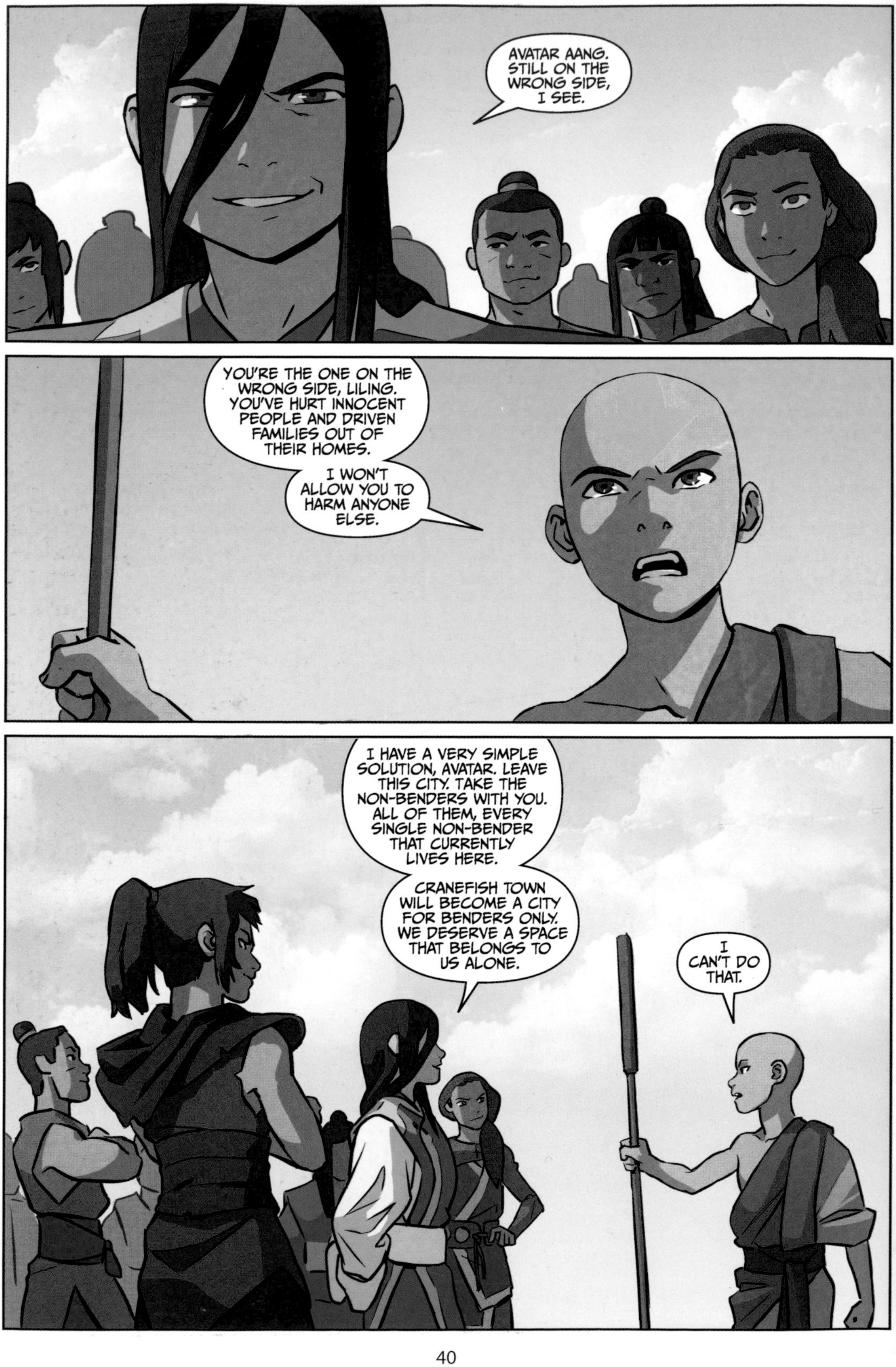
AVATAR AANG. STILL ON THE WRONG SIDE, I SEE.
YOU'RE THE ONE ON THE WRONG SIDE, LILING. YOU'VE HURT INNOCENT PEOPLE AND DRIVEN FAMILIES OUT OF THEIR HOMES.
I WON'T ALLOW YOU TO HARM ANYONE ELSE.
I HAVE A VERY SIMPLE SOLUTION, AVATAR. LEAVE THIS CITY. TAKE THE NON-BENDERS WITH YOU. ALL OF THEM, EVERY SINGLE NON-BENDER THAT CURRENTLY LIVES HERE.
CRANEFISH TOWN WILL BECOME A CITY FOR BENDERS ONLY. WE DESERVE A SPACE THAT BELONGS TO US ALONE.
I CAN'T DO THAT.

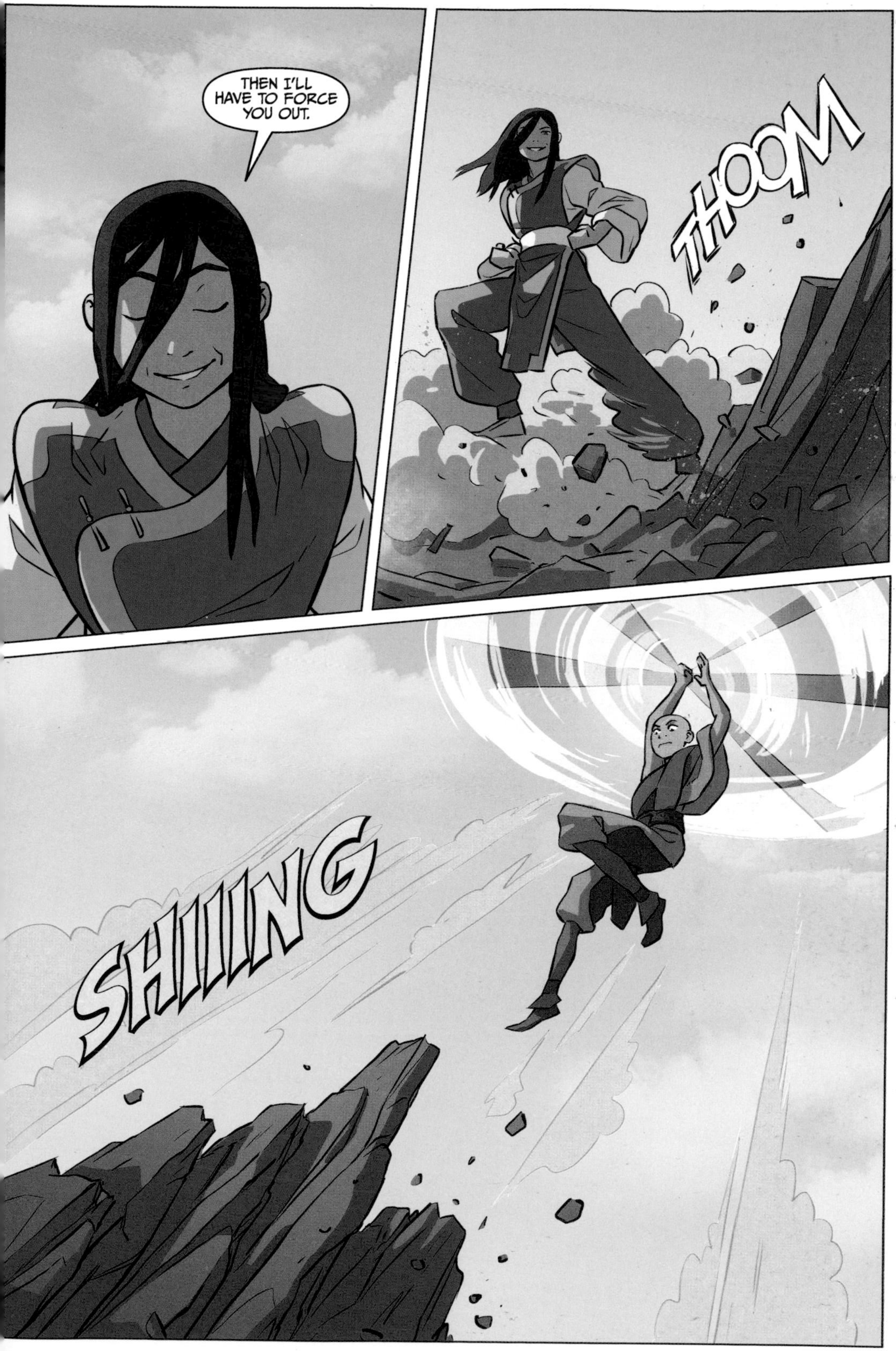
THEN I'LL HAVE TO FORCE YOU OUT.
THOOM
SHIIING

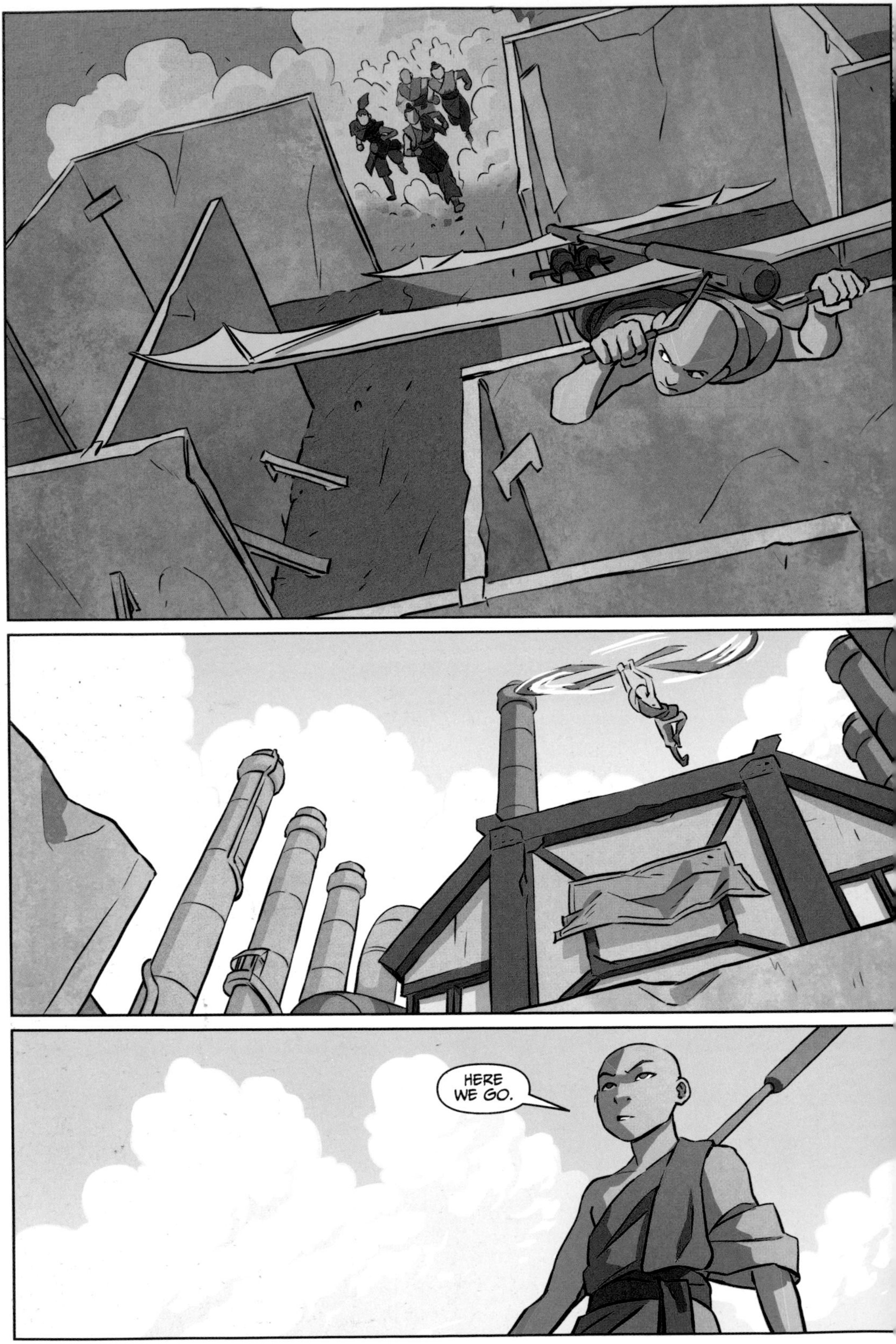
HERE WE GO.

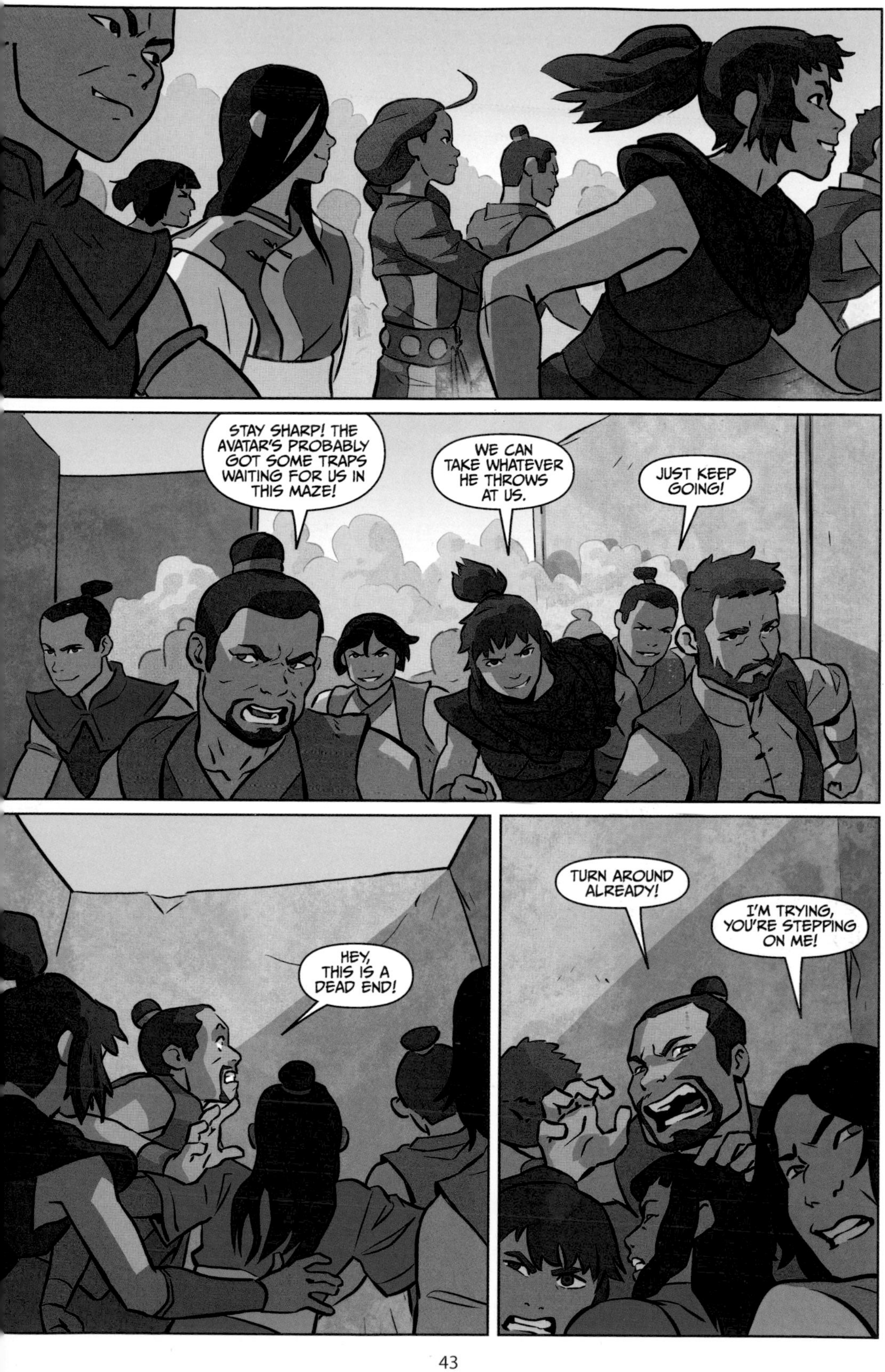
STAY SHARP! THE AVATAR'S PROBABLY GOT SOME TRAPS WAITING FOR US IN THIS MAZE!
WE CAN TAKE WHATEVER HE THROWS AT US.
JUST KEEP GOING!
HEY, THIS IS A DEAD END!
TURN AROUND ALREADY!
I'M TRYING, YOU'RE STEPPING ON ME!

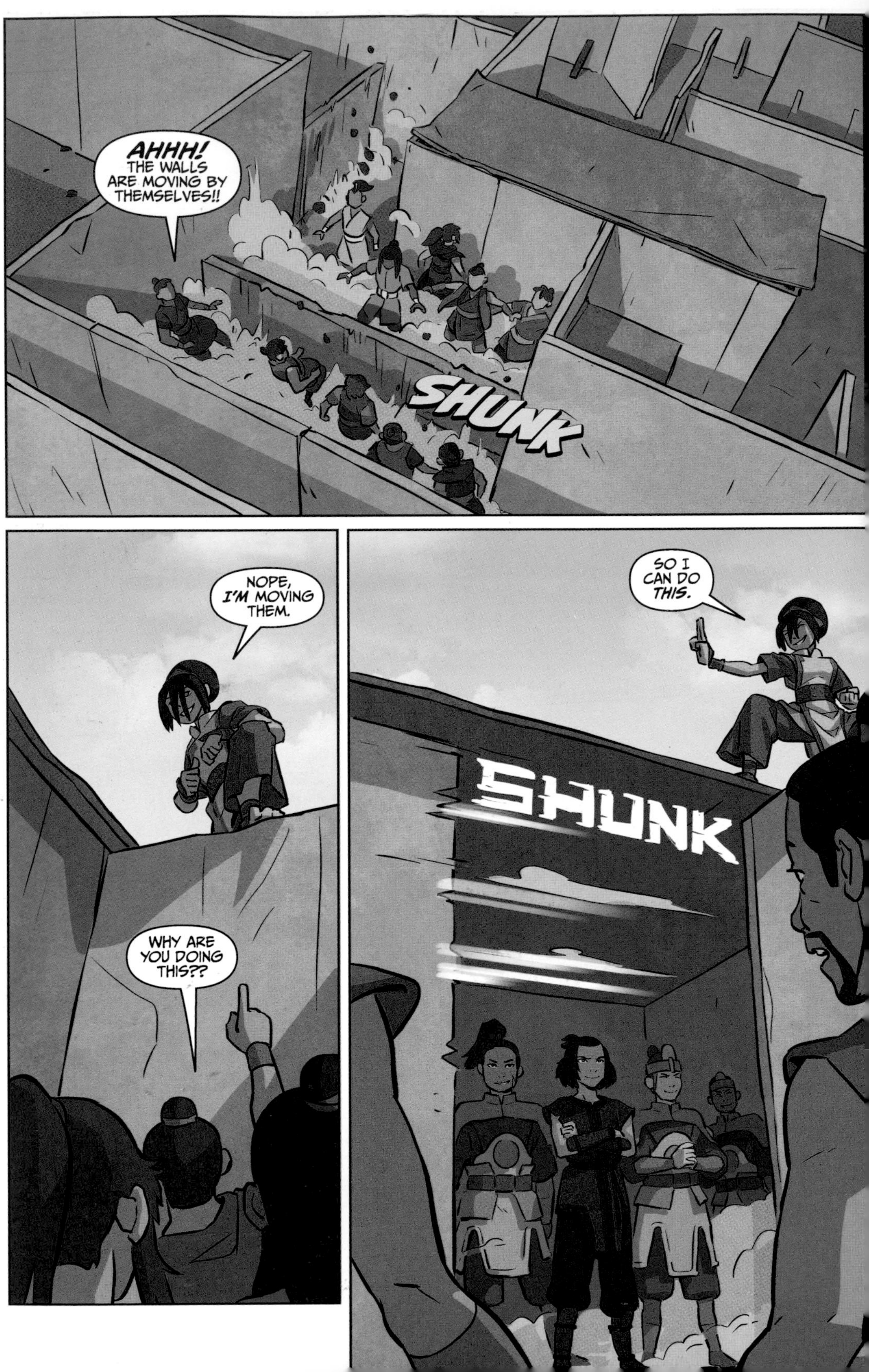
AHHH! THE WALLS ARE MOVING BY THEMSELVES!!
SHUNK
NOPE, I'M MOVING THEM.
WHY ARE YOU DOING THIS??
SO I CAN DO THIS.
SHUNK

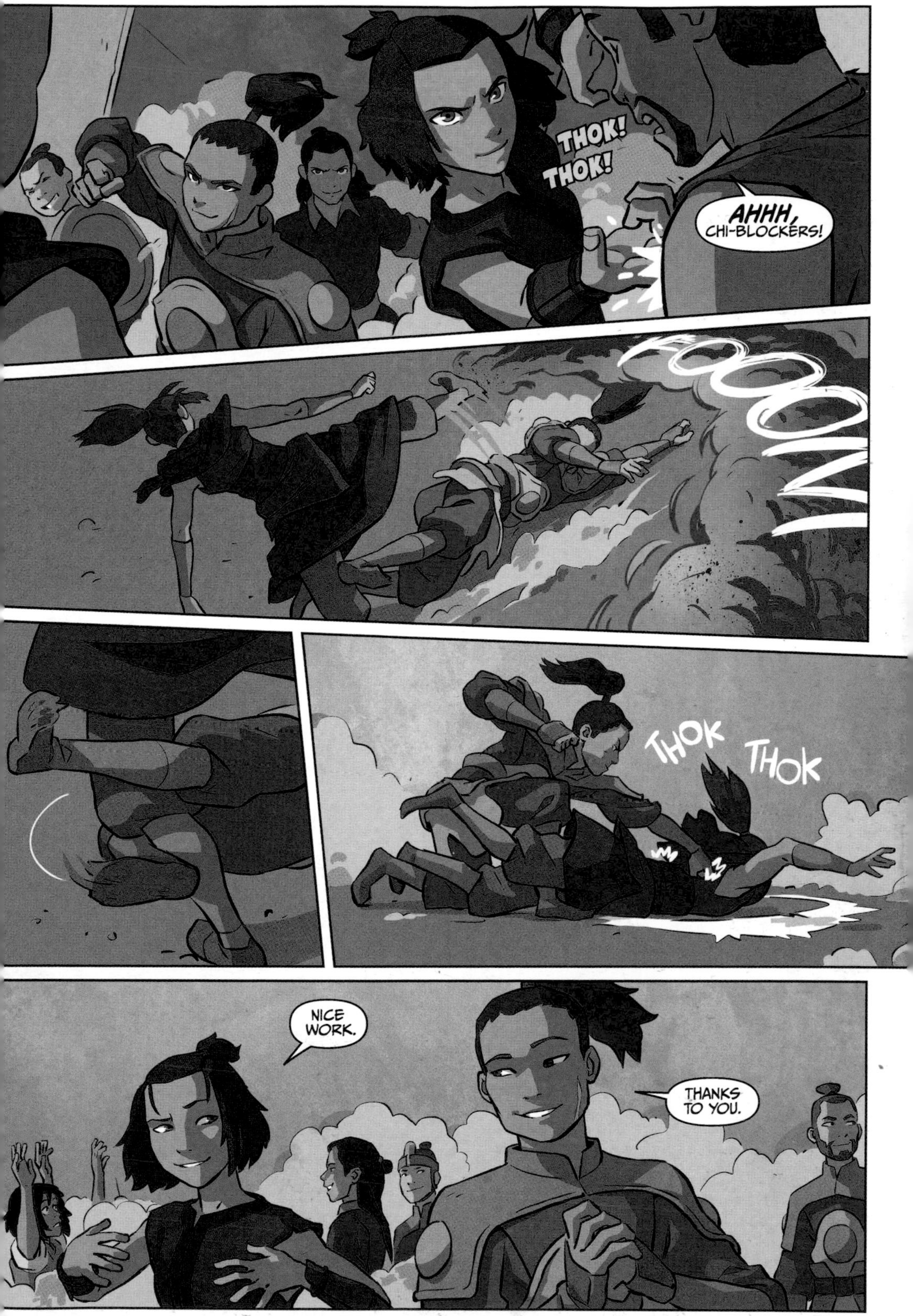
THOK!
THOK!
AHHH, CHI-BLOCKERS!
FOOOOM!
THOK
THOK
NICE WORK.
THANKS TO YOU.

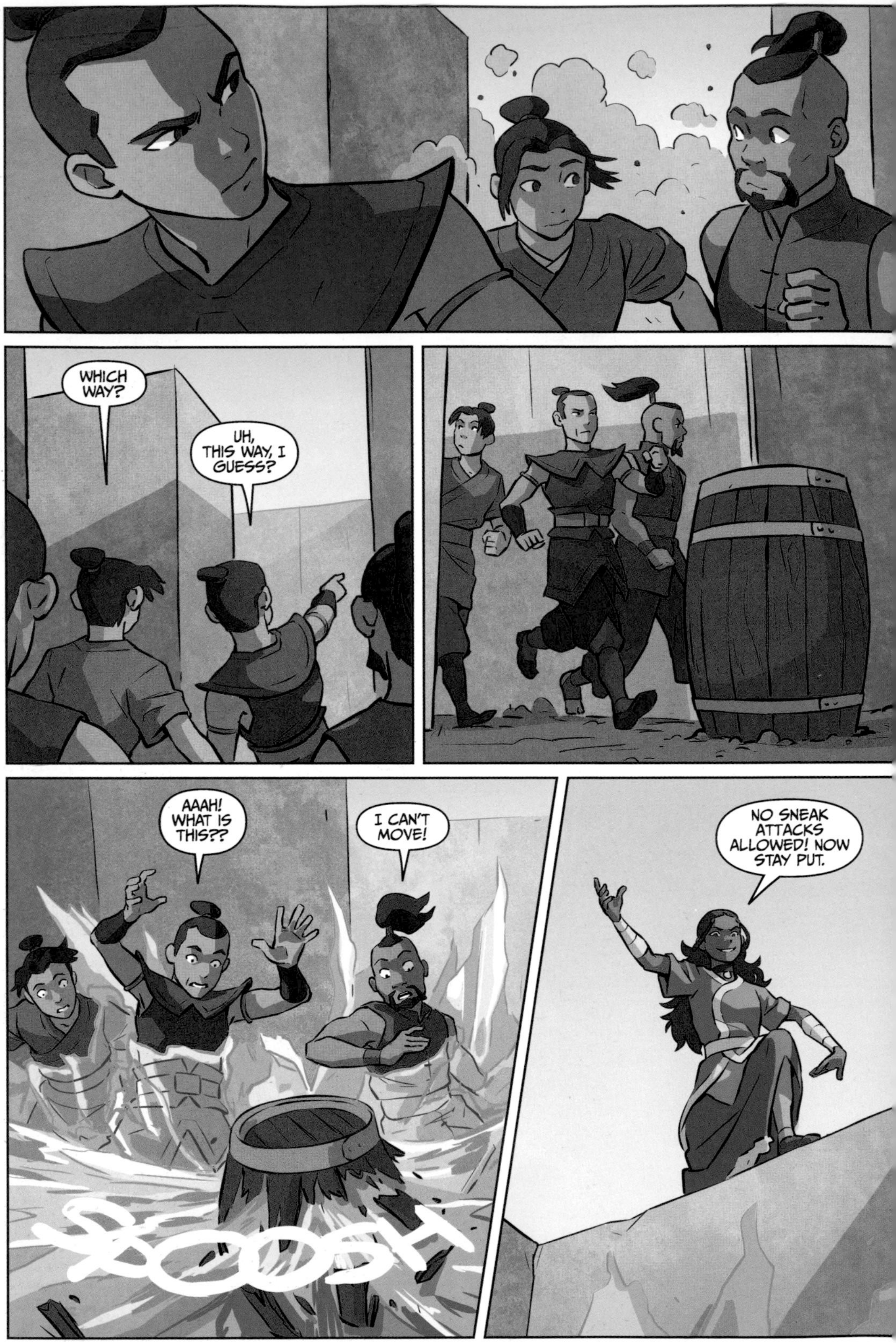
WHICH WAY?
UH, THIS WAY, I GUESS?
AAAH! WHAT IS THIS??
I CAN'T MOVE!
SOOSH
NO SNEAK ATTACKS ALLOWED! NOW STAY PUT.

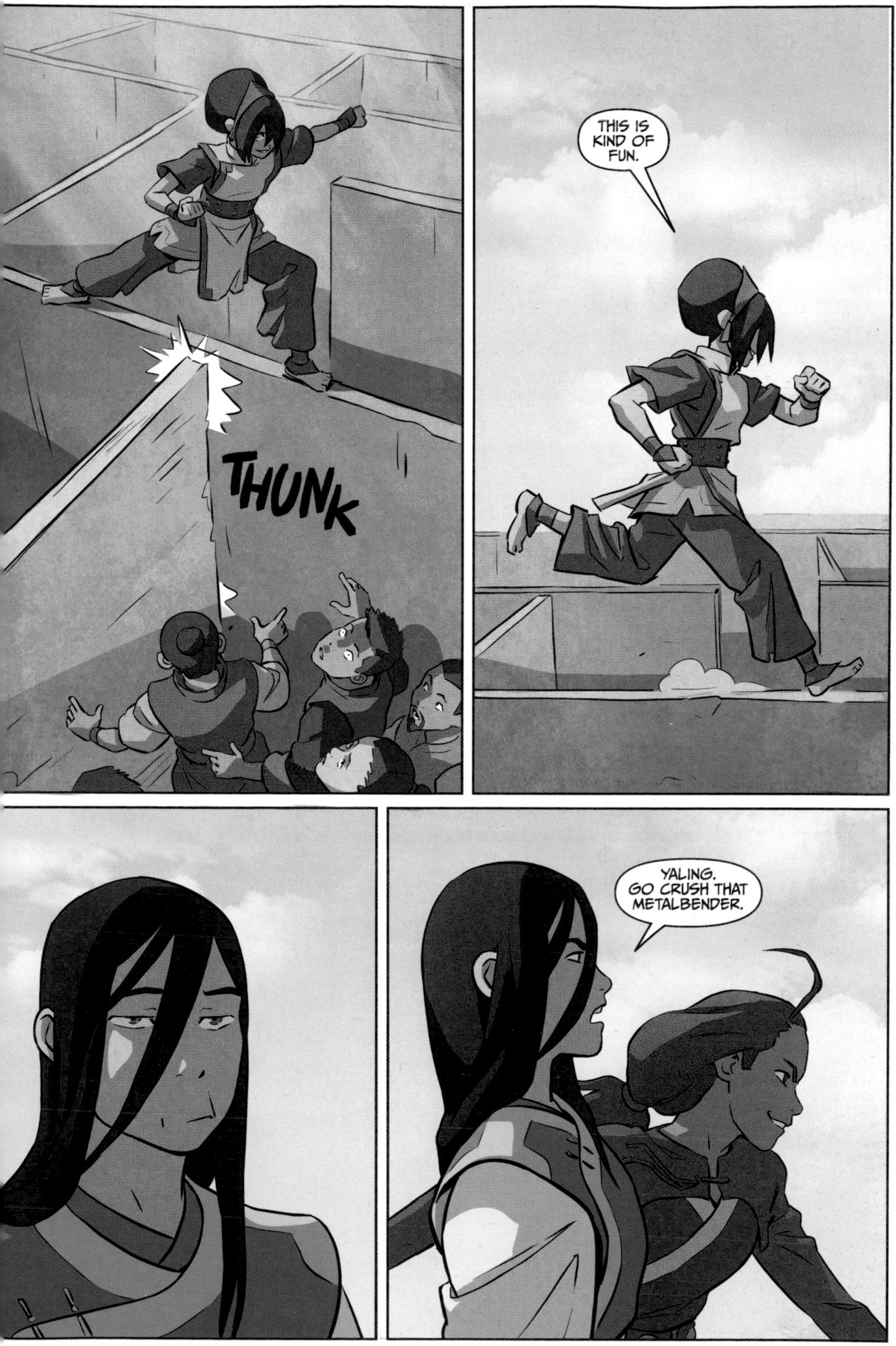
THUNK
THIS IS KIND OF FUN.
YALING. GO CRUSH THAT METALBENDER.

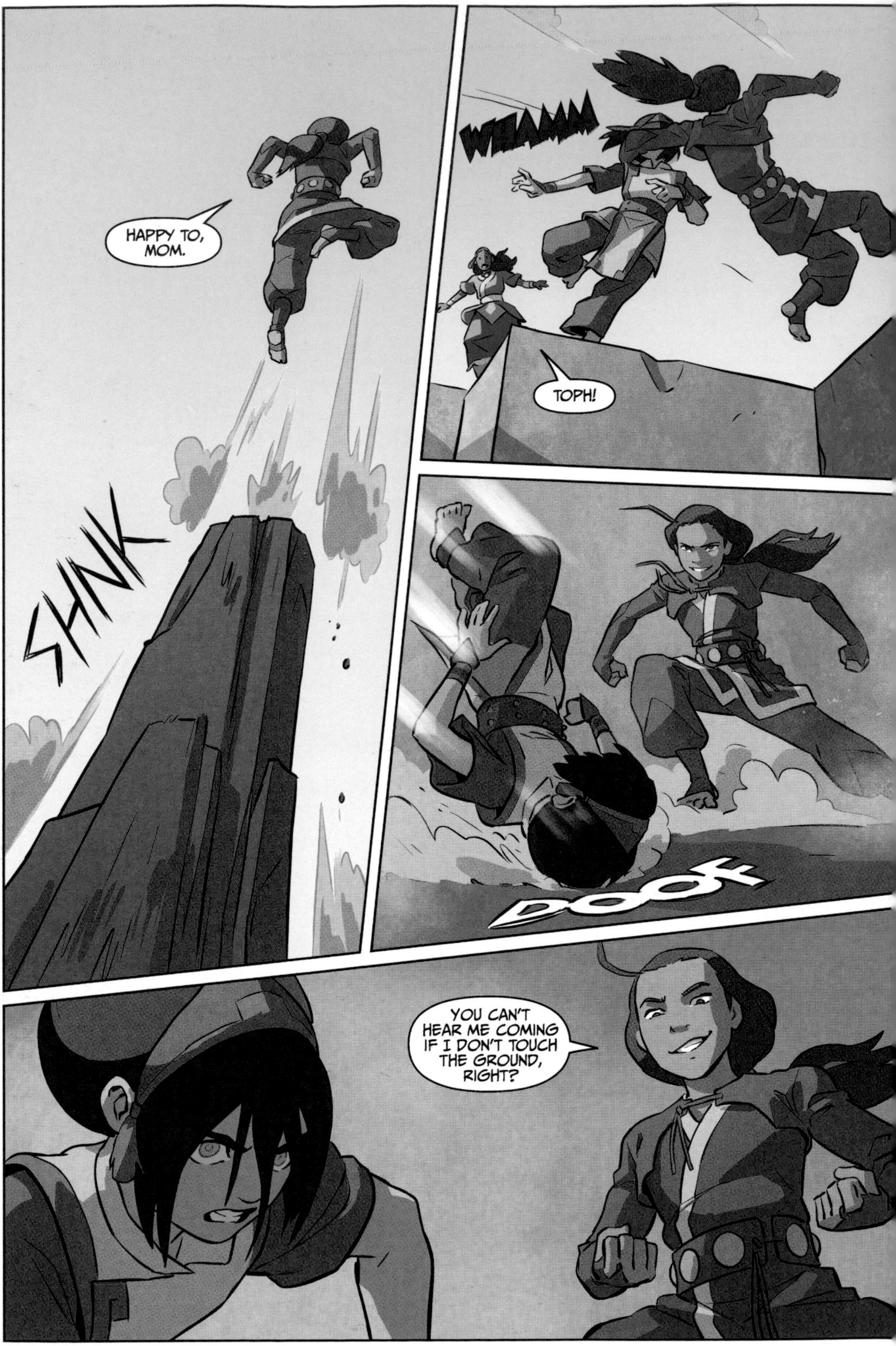
HAPPY TO, MOM.
WHAMM
TOPH!
SHNK
DOOF
YOU CAN'T HEAR ME COMING IF I DON'T TOUCH THE GROUND, RIGHT?

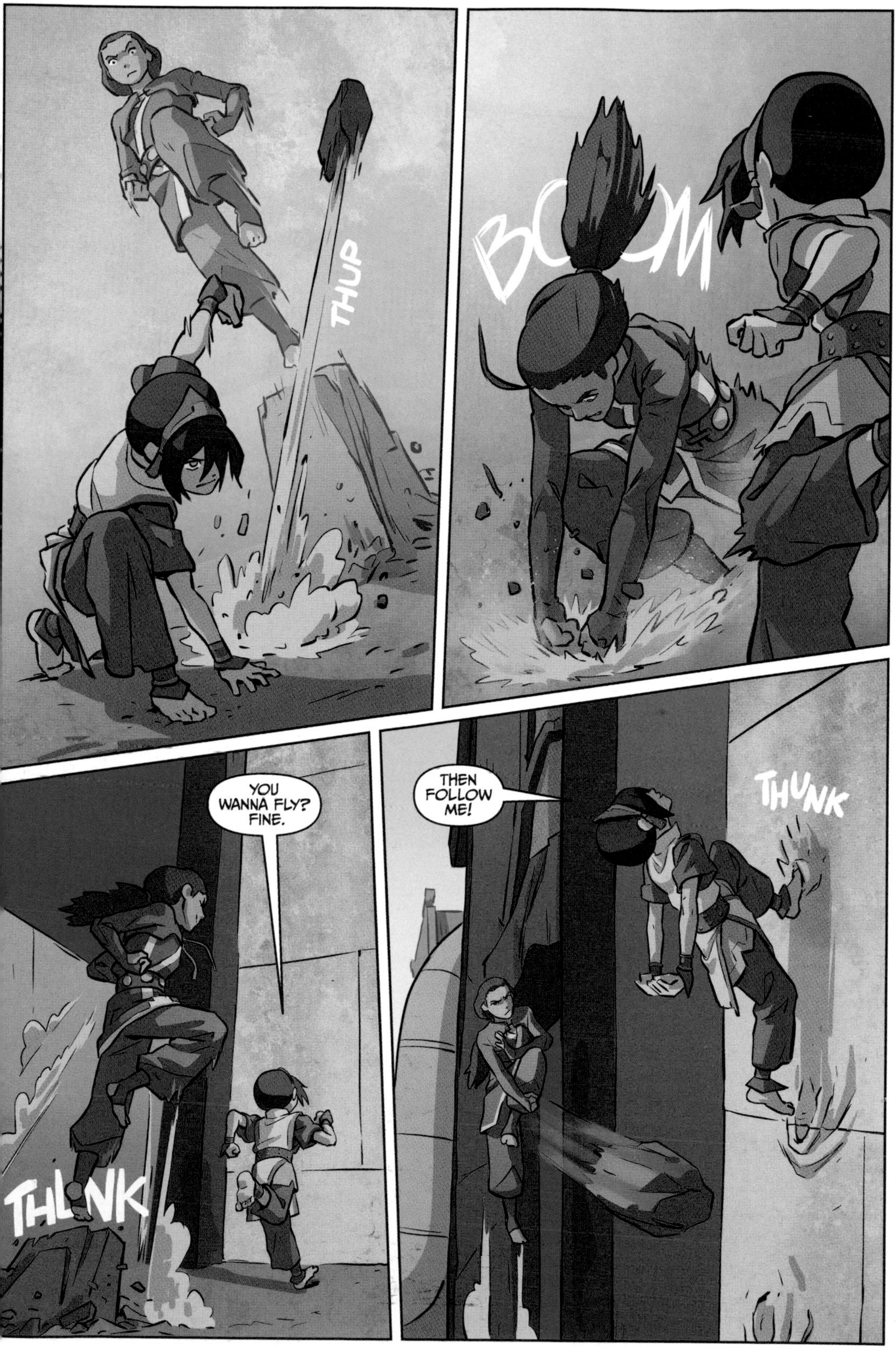
THUP
BOOM
YOU WANNA FLY? FINE.
THUNK
THEN FOLLOW ME!
THUNK

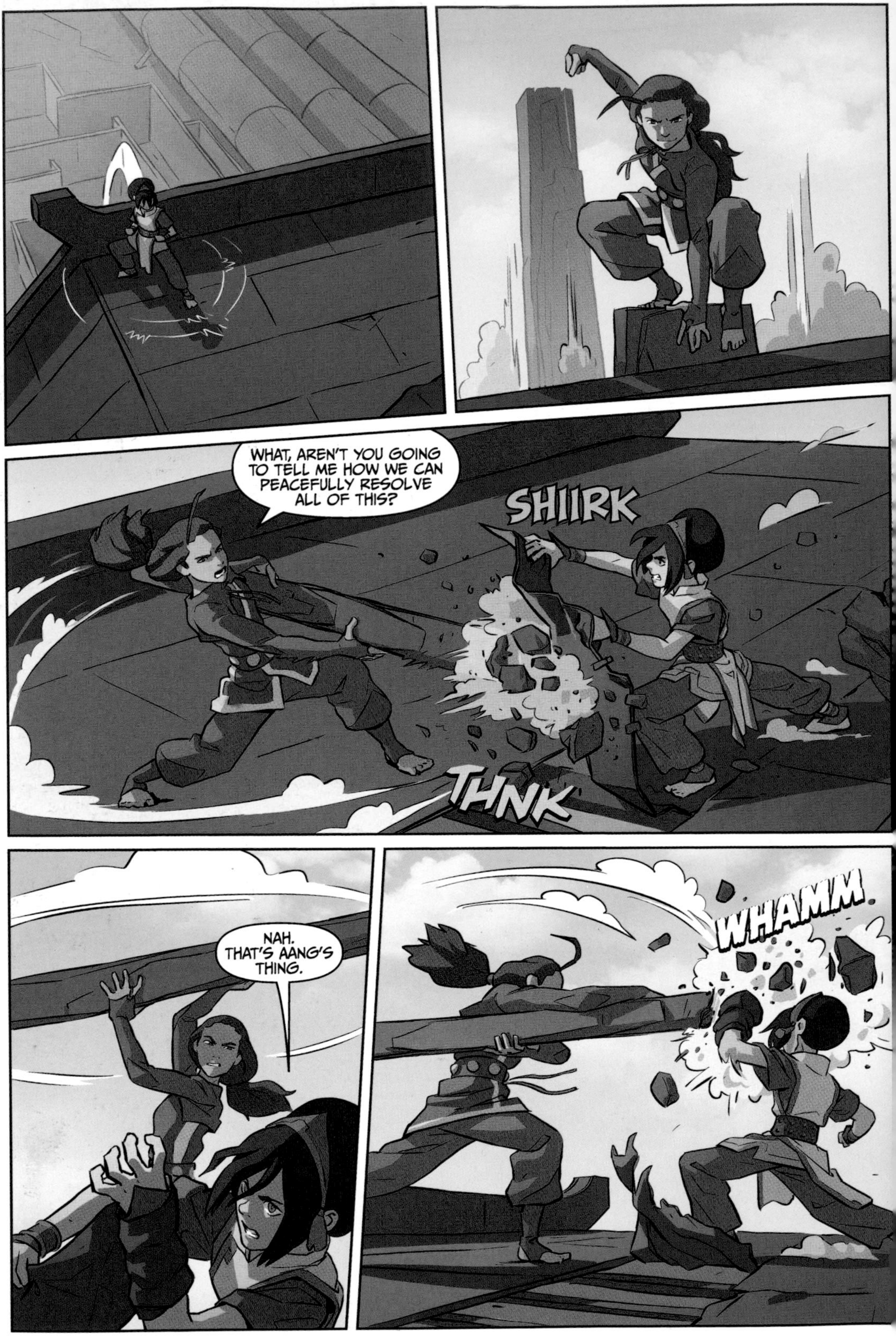
WHAT, AREN'T YOU GOING TO TELL ME HOW WE CAN PEACEFULLY RESOLVE ALL OF THIS?
SHIIRK
THNK
NAH. THAT'S AANG'S THING.
WHAMM

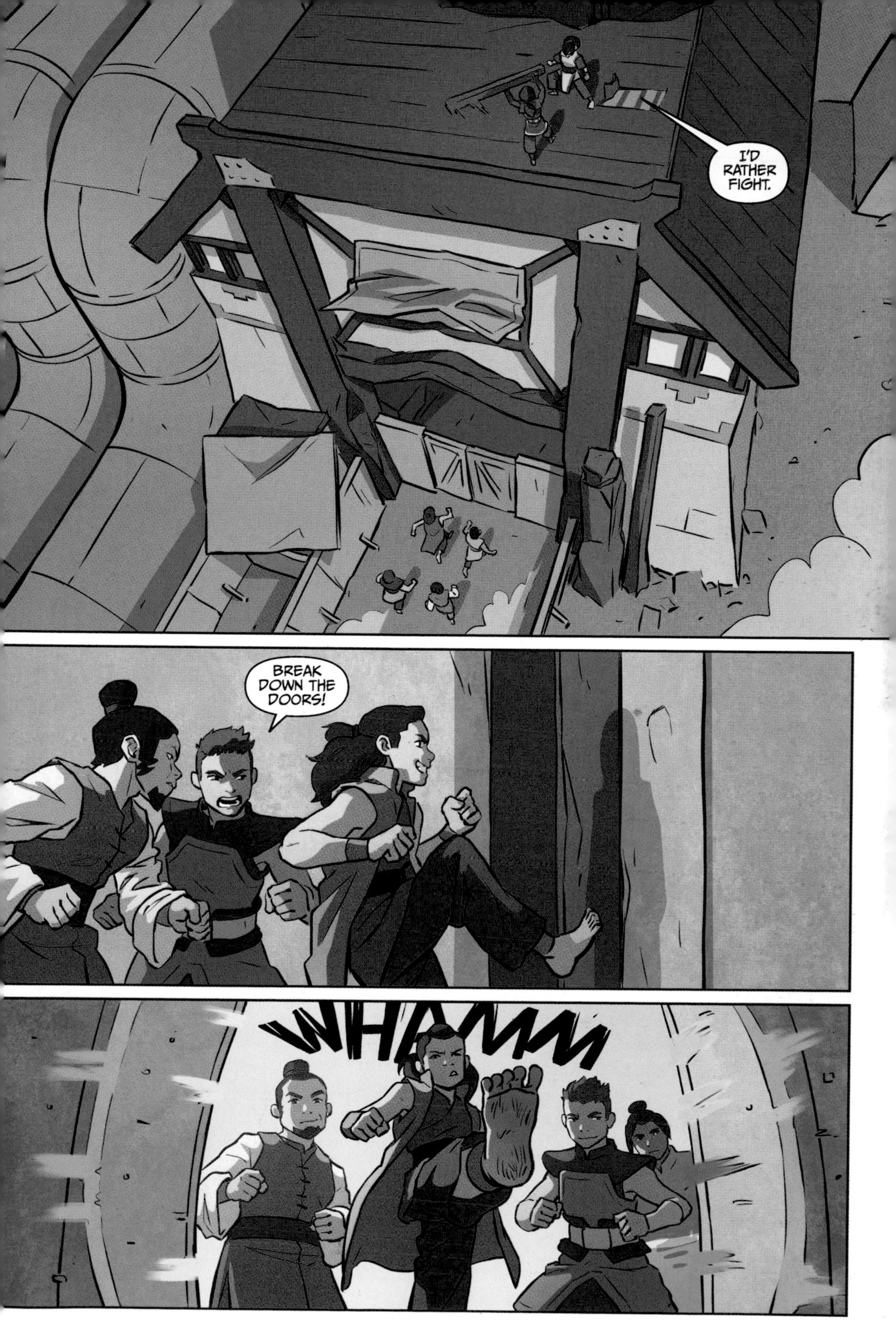
I'D RATHER FIGHT.
BREAK DOWN THE DOORS!
WHAMM

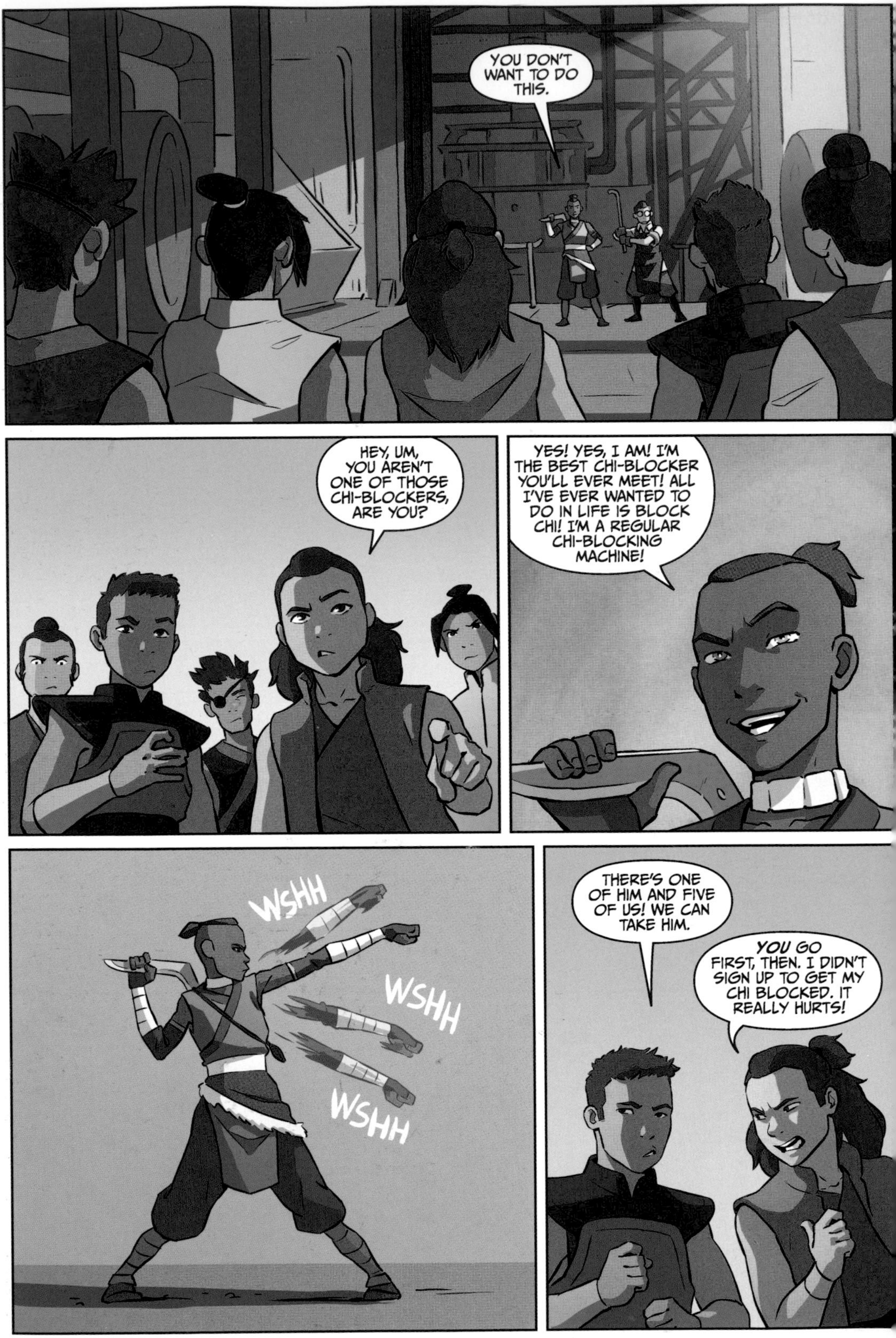

YOU DON'T WANT TO DO THIS.
HEY, UM, YOU AREN'T ONE OF THOSE CHI-BLOCKERS, ARE YOU?
YES! YES, I AM! I'M THE BEST CHI-BLOCKER YOU'LL EVER MEET! ALL I'VE EVER WANTED TO DO IN LIFE IS BLOCK CHI! I'M A REGULAR CHI-BLOCKING MACHINE!
WSHH
WSHH
WSHH
THERE'S ONE OF HIM AND FIVE OF US! WE CAN TAKE HIM.
YOU GO FIRST, THEN. I DIDN'T SIGN UP TO GET MY CHI BLOCKED. IT REALLY HURTS!

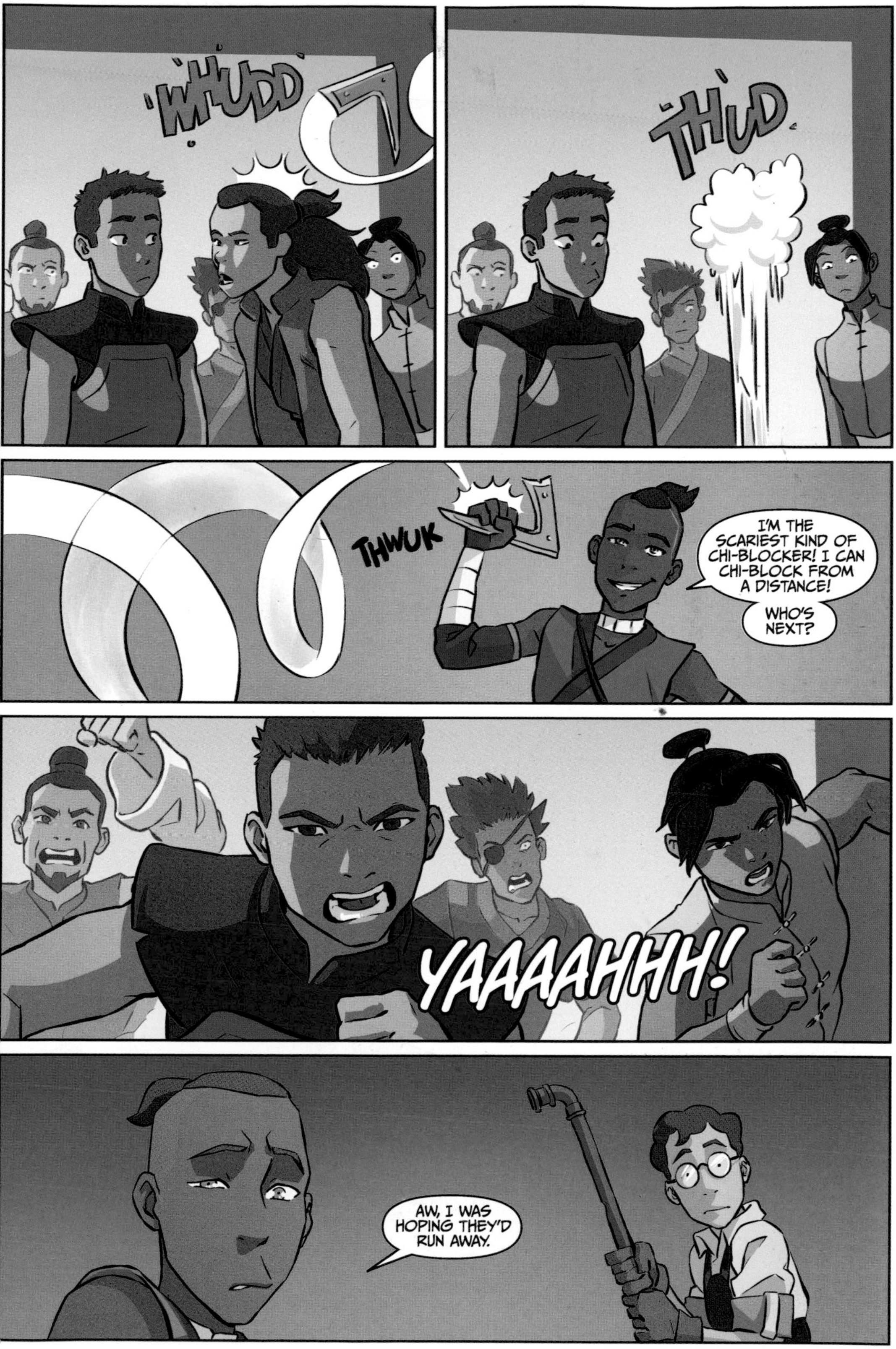
WHUDD
THUD
THWUK
I'M THE SCARIEST KIND OF CHI-BLOCKER! I CAN CHI-BLOCK FROM A DISTANCE!
WHO'S NEXT?
YAAAAHHH!
AW, I WAS HOPING THEY'D RUN AWAY.

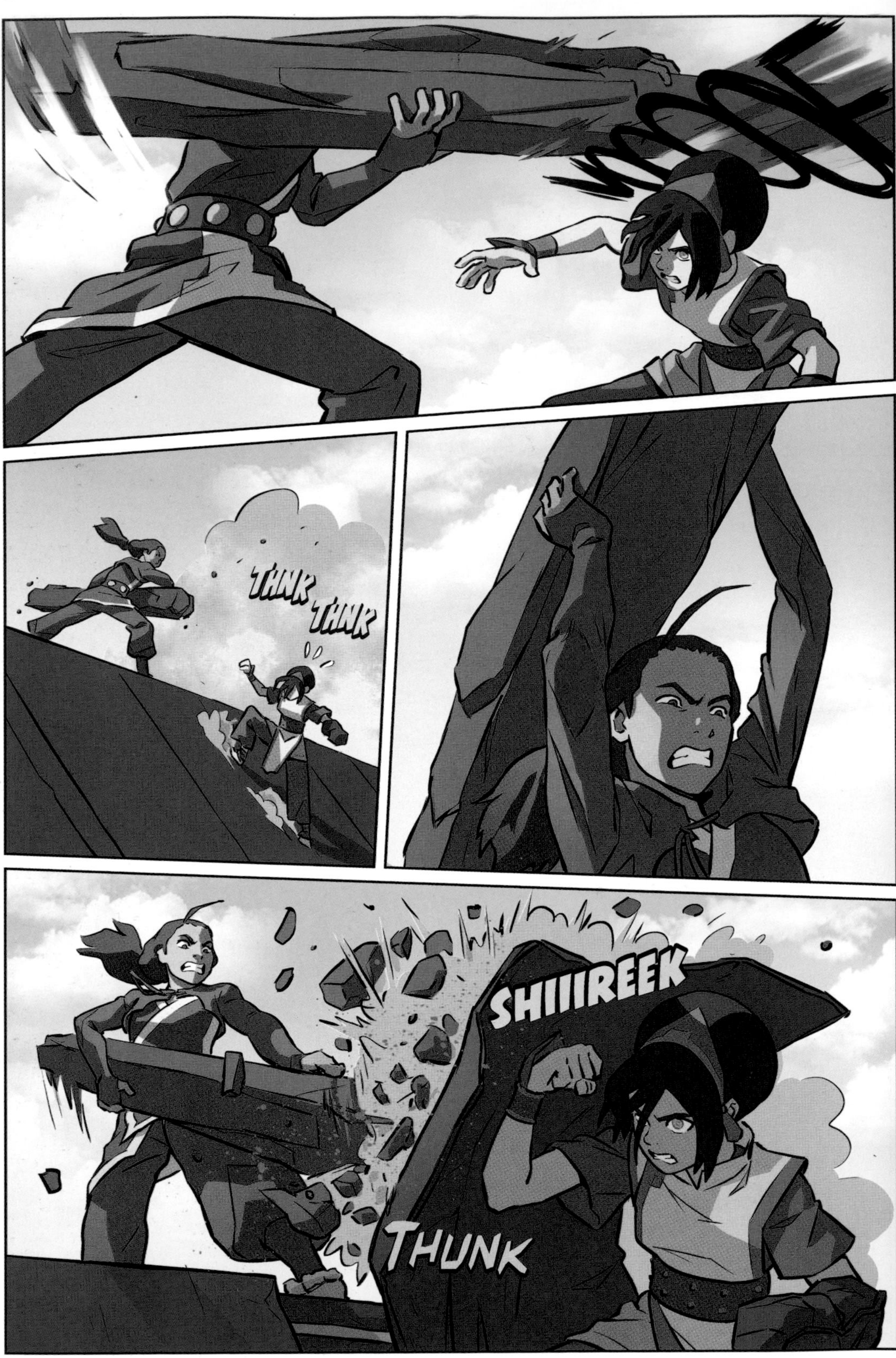
THNK
THNK
SHIIIREEK
THUNK

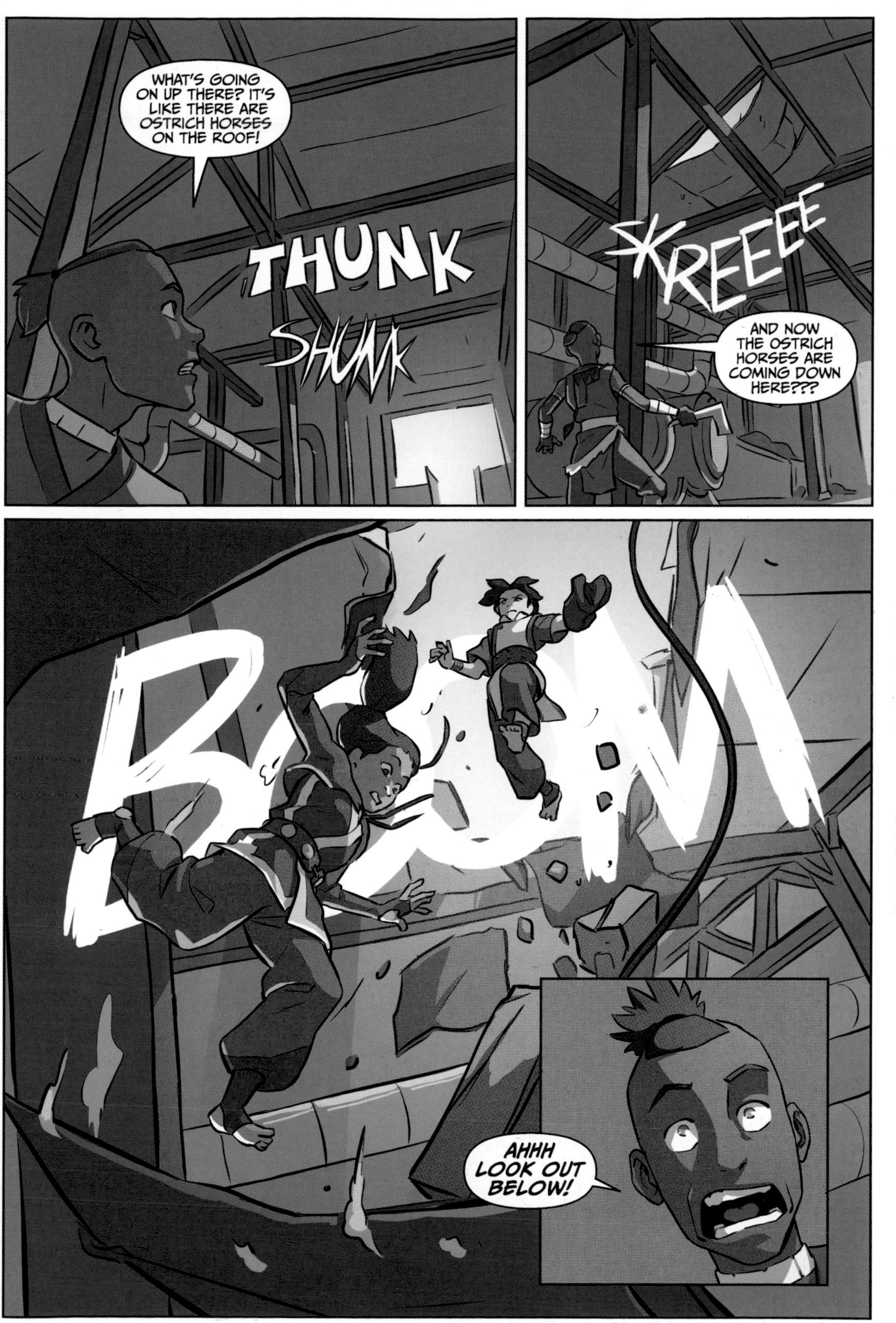
WHAT'S GOING ON UP THERE? IT'S LIKE THERE ARE OSTRICH HORSES ON THE ROOF!
THUNK
SHUNK
SKREEEE
AND NOW THE OSTRICH HORSES ARE COMING DOWN HERE???
BOOM
AHHH LOOK OUT BELOW!

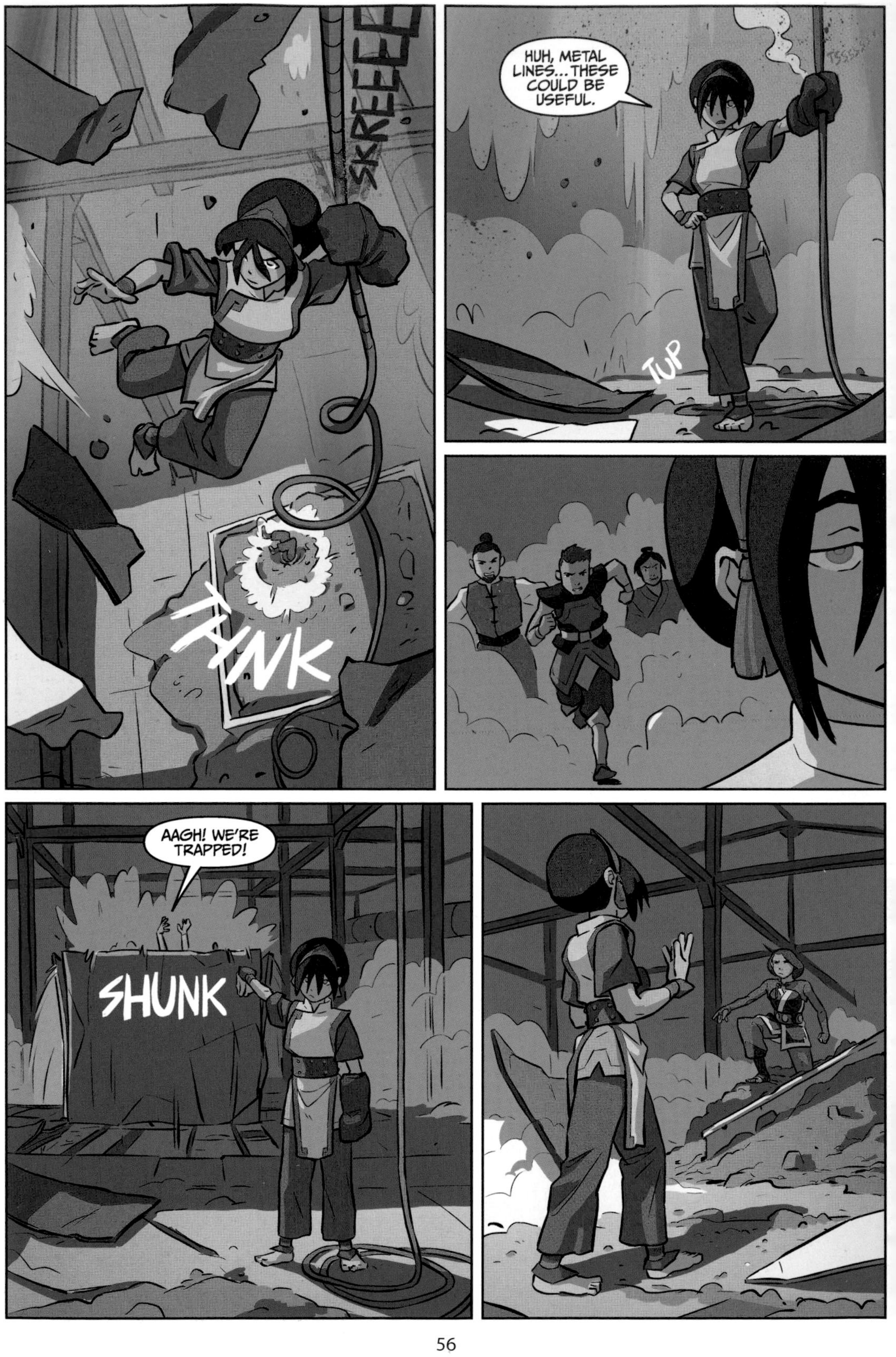
SKREEEE
THNK
HUH, METAL LINES... THESE COULD BE USEFUL.
TUP
AAGH! WE'RE TRAPPED!
SHUNK

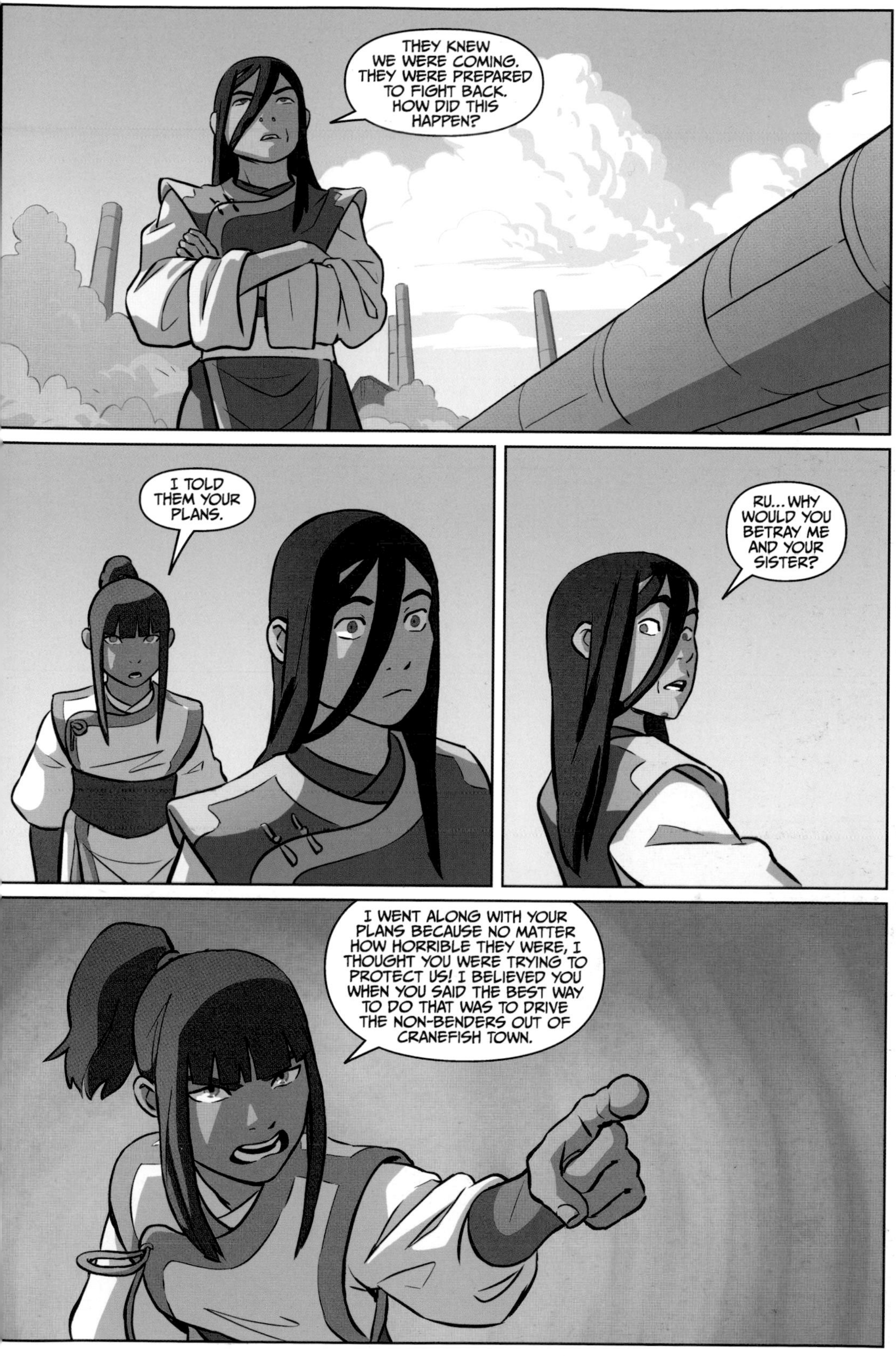
THEY KNEW WE WERE COMING. THEY WERE PREPARED TO FIGHT BACK. HOW DID THIS HAPPEN?
I TOLD THEM YOUR PLANS.
RU... WHY WOULD YOU BETRAY ME AND YOUR SISTER?
I WENT ALONG WITH YOUR PLANS BECAUSE NO MATTER HOW HORRIBLE THEY WERE, I THOUGHT YOU WERE TRYING TO PROTECT US! I BELIEVED YOU WHEN YOU SAID THE BEST WAY TO DO THAT WAS TO DRIVE THE NON-BENDERS OUT OF CRANEFISH TOWN.

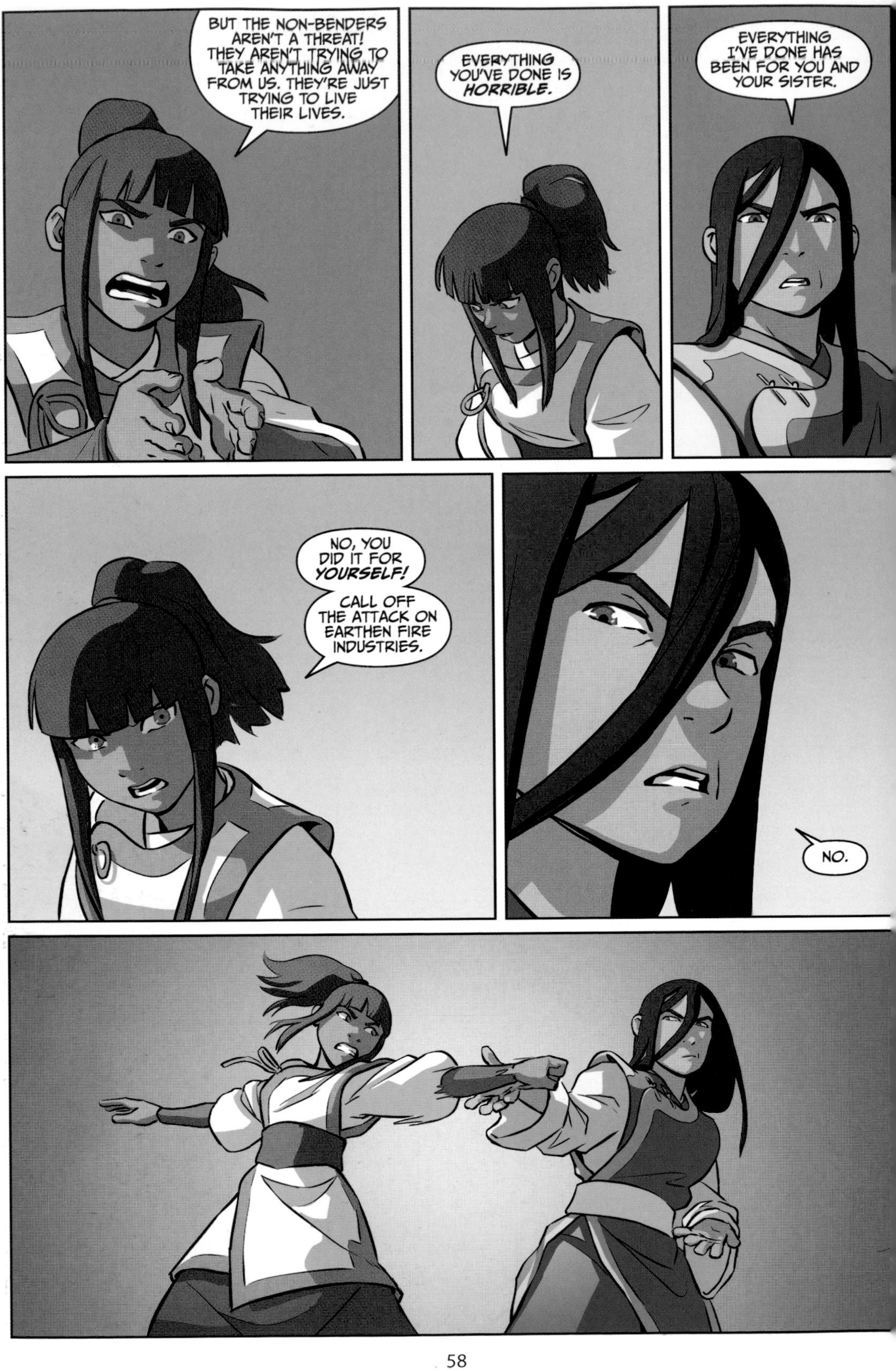
BUT THE NON-BENDERS AREN'T A THREAT! THEY AREN'T TRYING TO TAKE ANYTHING AWAY FROM US. THEY'RE JUST TRYING TO LIVE THEIR LIVES.
EVERYTHING YOU'VE DONE IS *HORRIBLE.*
EVERYTHING I'VE DONE HAS BEEN FOR YOU AND YOUR SISTER.
NO, YOU DID IT FOR *YOURSELF!*
CALL OFF THE ATTACK ON EARTHEN FIRE INDUSTRIES.
NO.

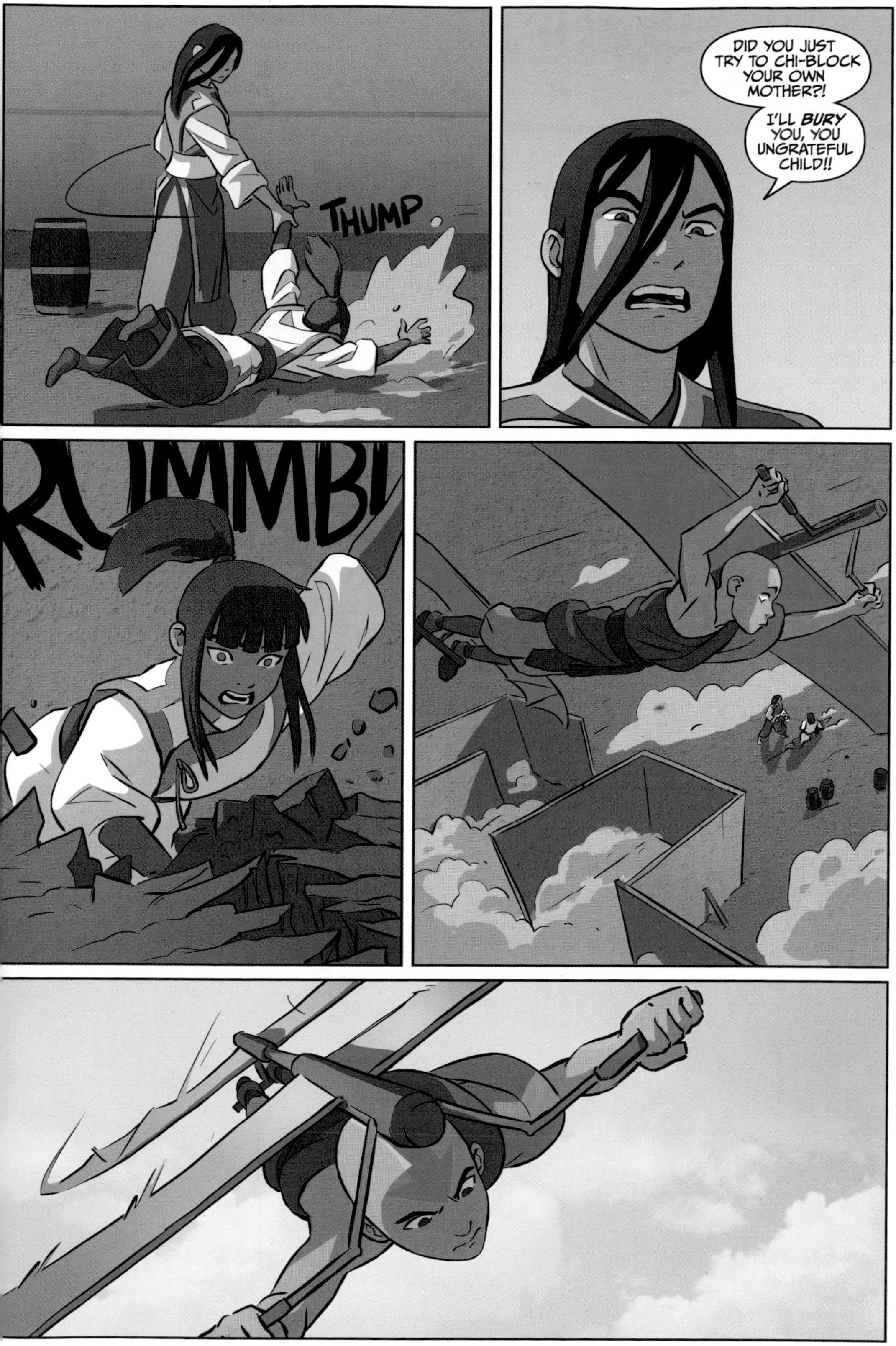
THUMP
DID YOU JUST TRY TO CHI-BLOCK YOUR OWN MOTHER?!
I'LL BURY YOU, YOU UNGRATEFUL CHILD!!
RUMMBL

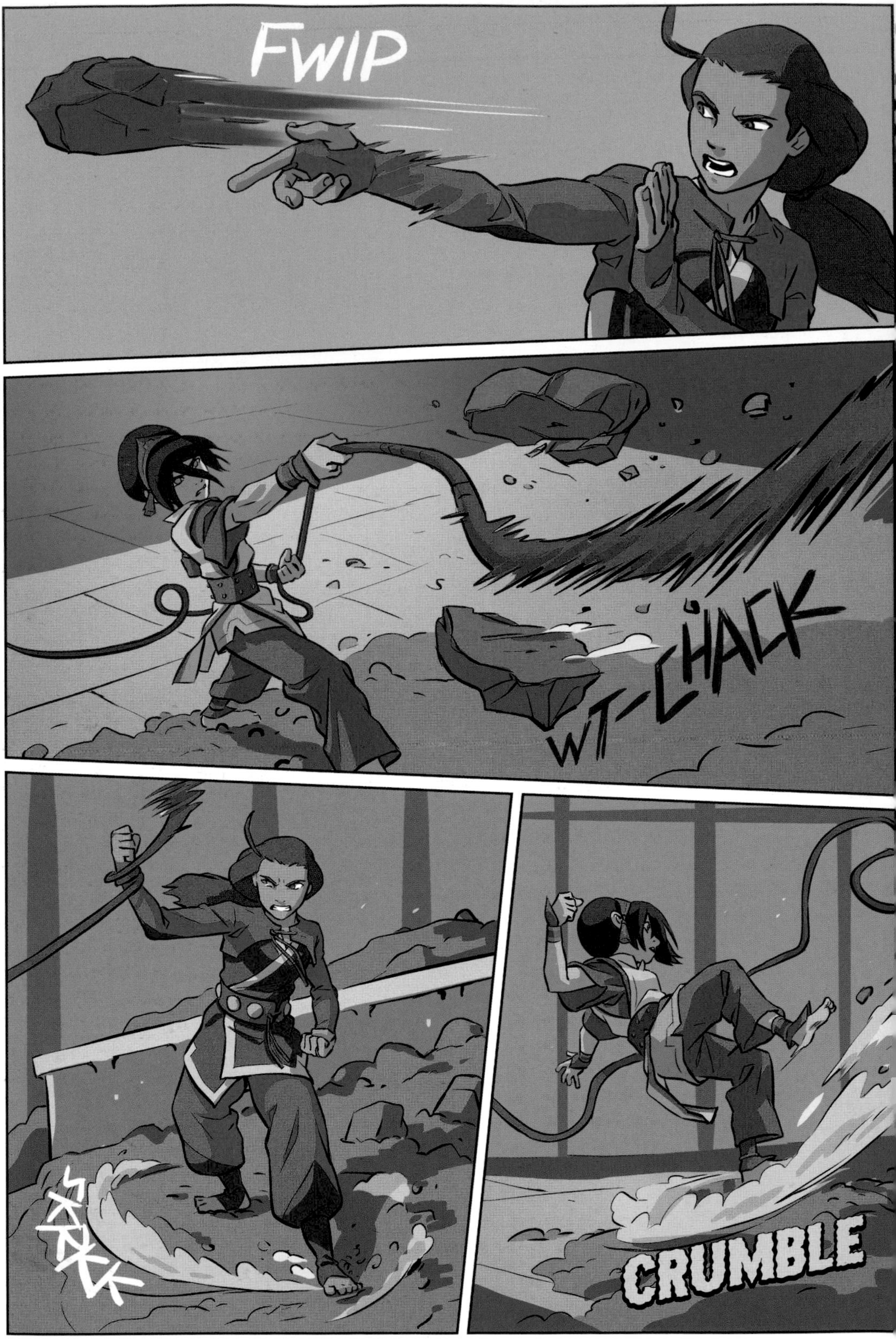
FWIP
WT-CHACK
SKRKK
CRUMBLE

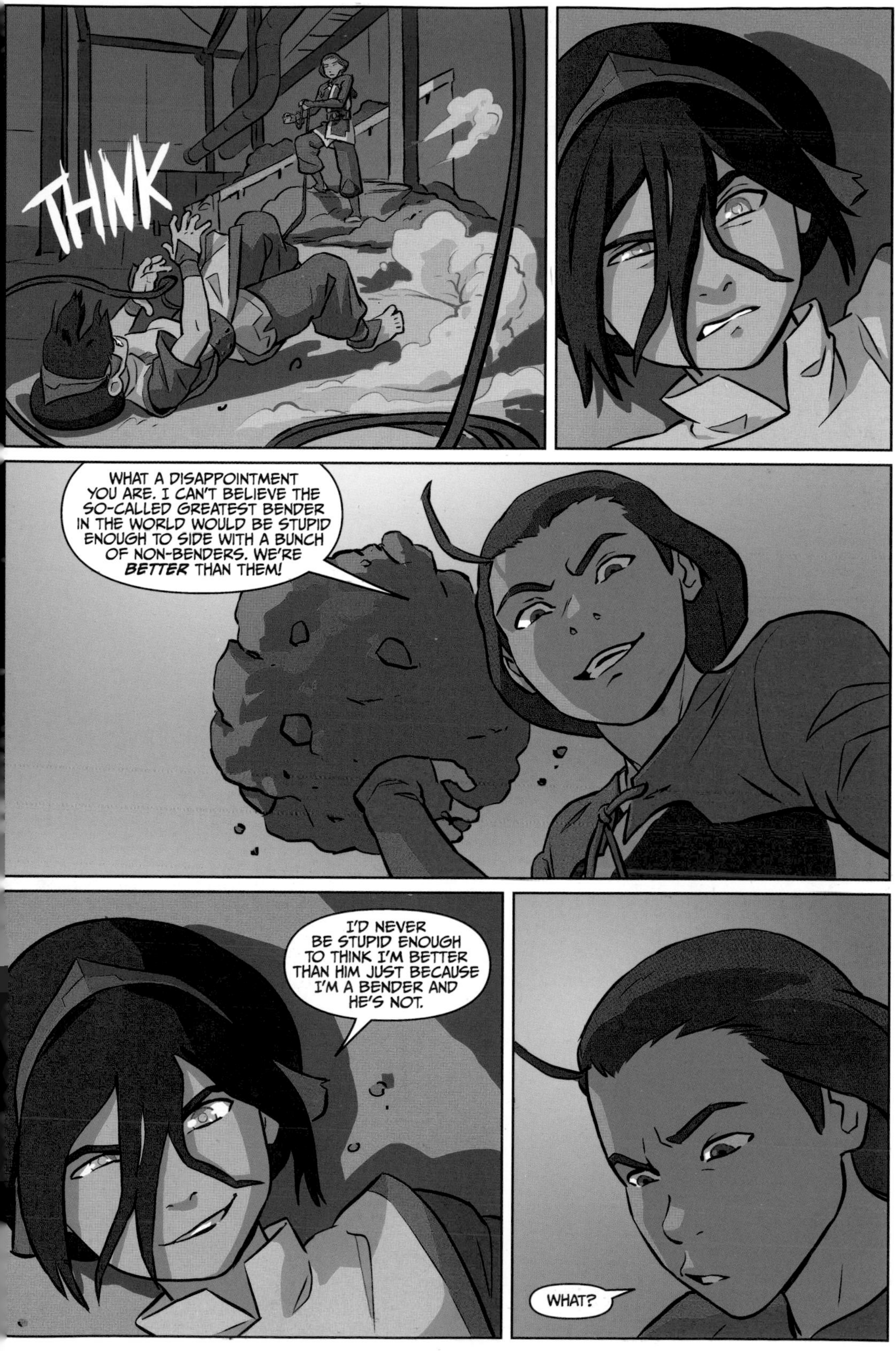
THNK
WHAT A DISAPPOINTMENT YOU ARE. I CAN'T BELIEVE THE SO-CALLED GREATEST BENDER IN THE WORLD WOULD BE STUPID ENOUGH TO SIDE WITH A BUNCH OF NON-BENDERS. WE'RE *BETTER* THAN THEM!
I'D NEVER BE STUPID ENOUGH TO THINK I'M BETTER THAN HIM JUST BECAUSE I'M A BENDER AND HE'S NOT.
WHAT?

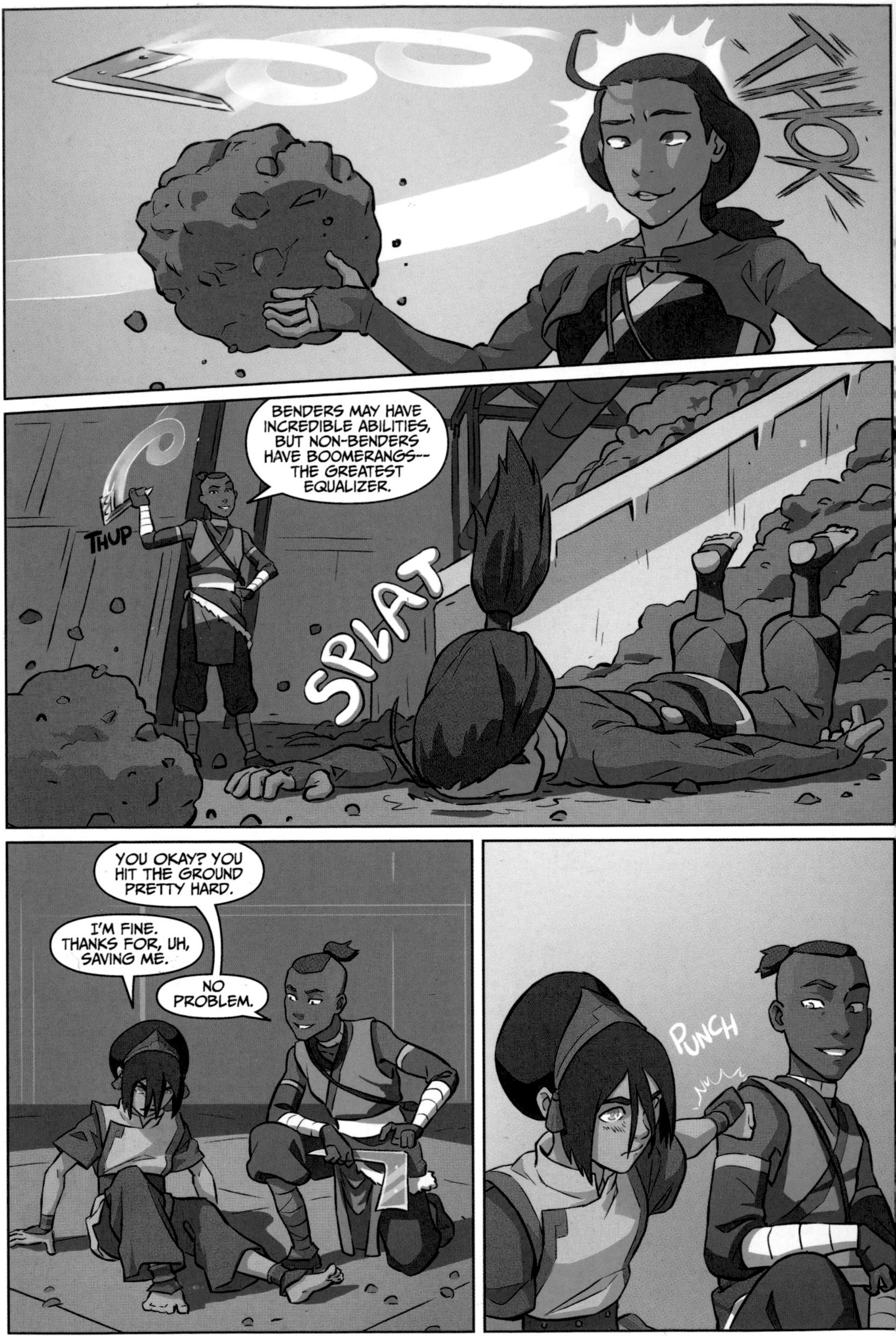
THOK
BENDERS MAY HAVE INCREDIBLE ABILITIES, BUT NON-BENDERS HAVE BOOMERANGS-- THE GREATEST EQUALIZER.
THUP
SPLAT
YOU OKAY? YOU HIT THE GROUND PRETTY HARD.
I'M FINE. THANKS FOR, UH, SAVING ME.
NO PROBLEM.
PUNCH

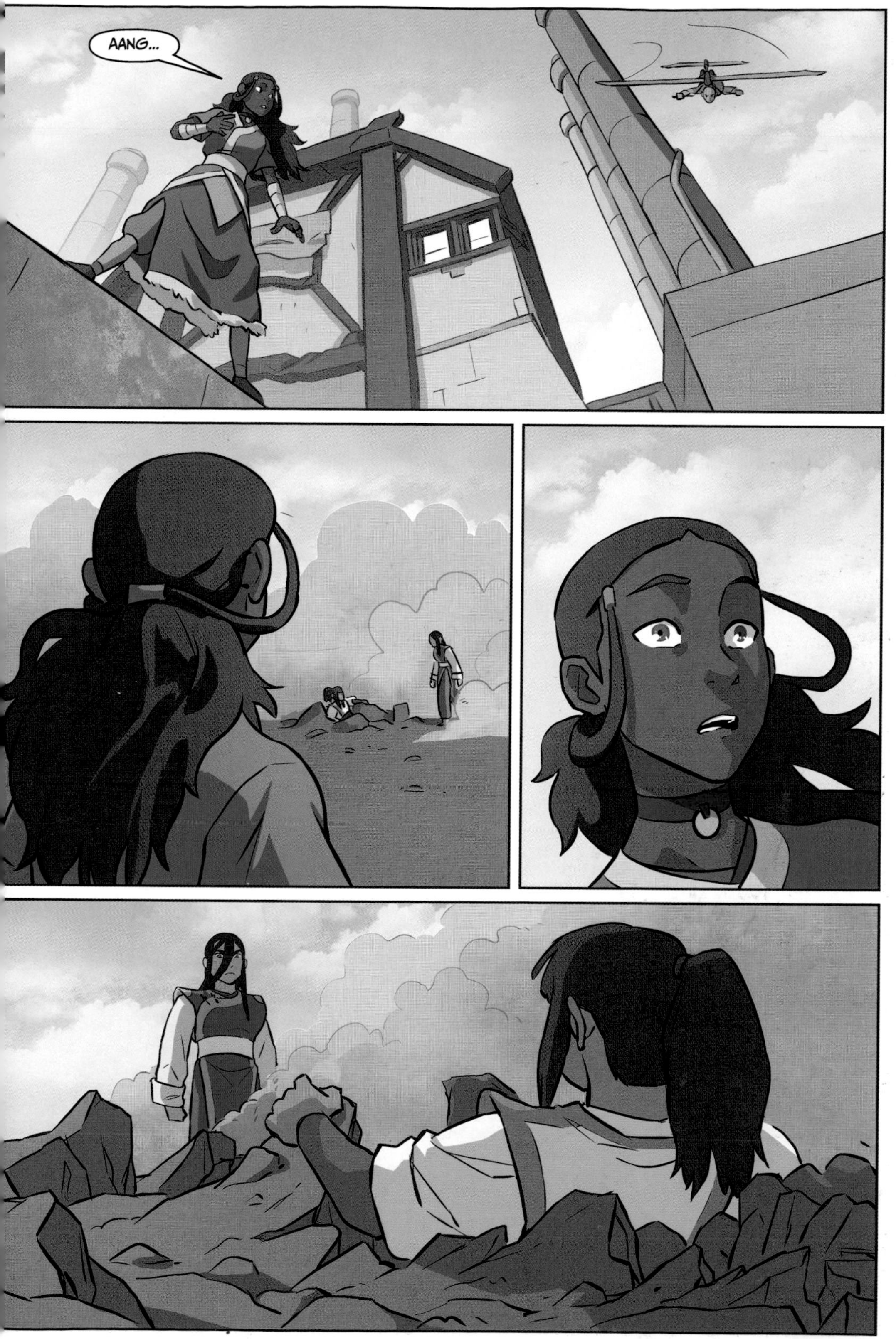
AANG...

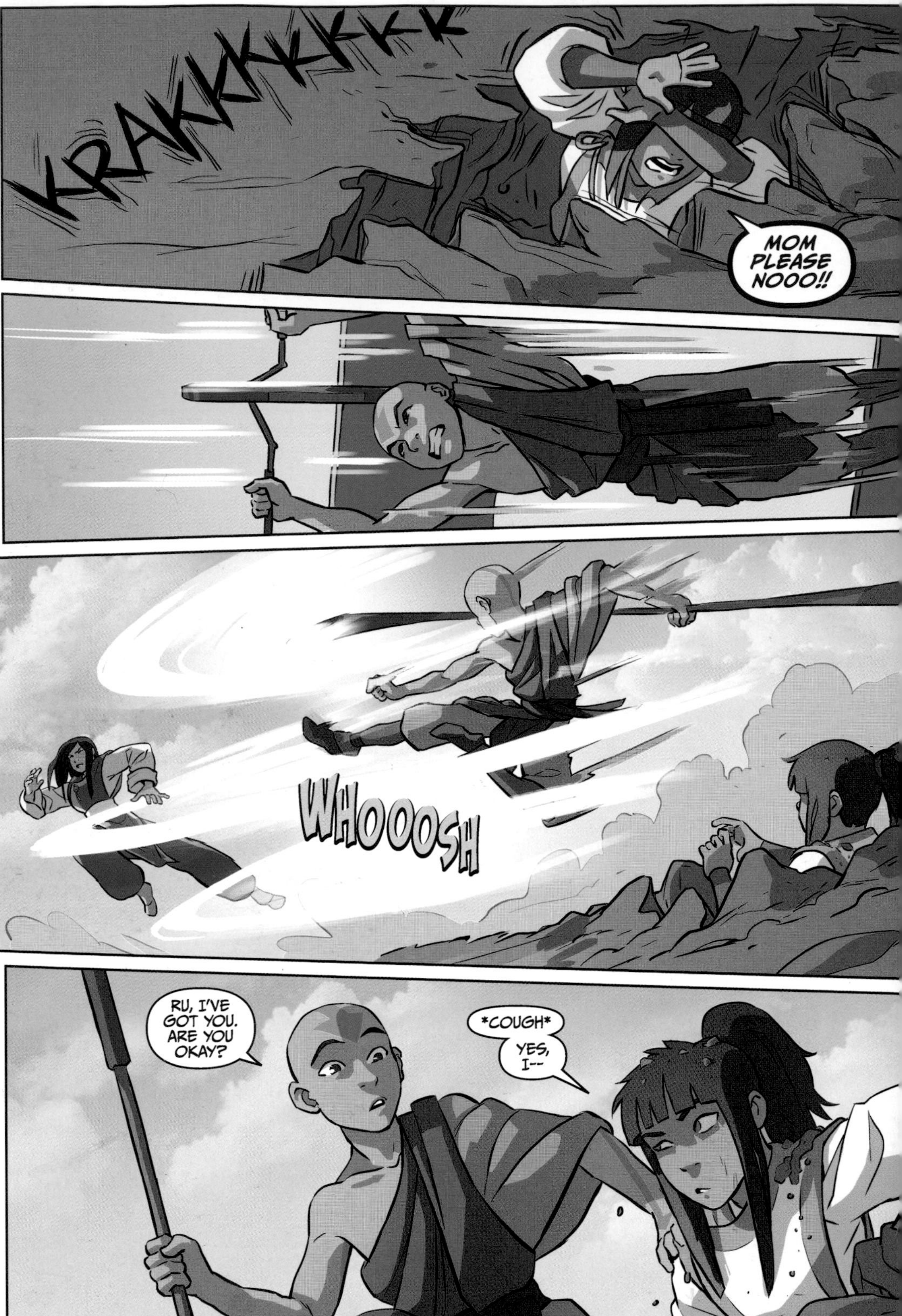
KRAKKKKKKK
MOM PLEASE NOOO!!
WHOOOSH
RU, I'VE GOT YOU. ARE YOU OKAY?
COUGH
YES, I--

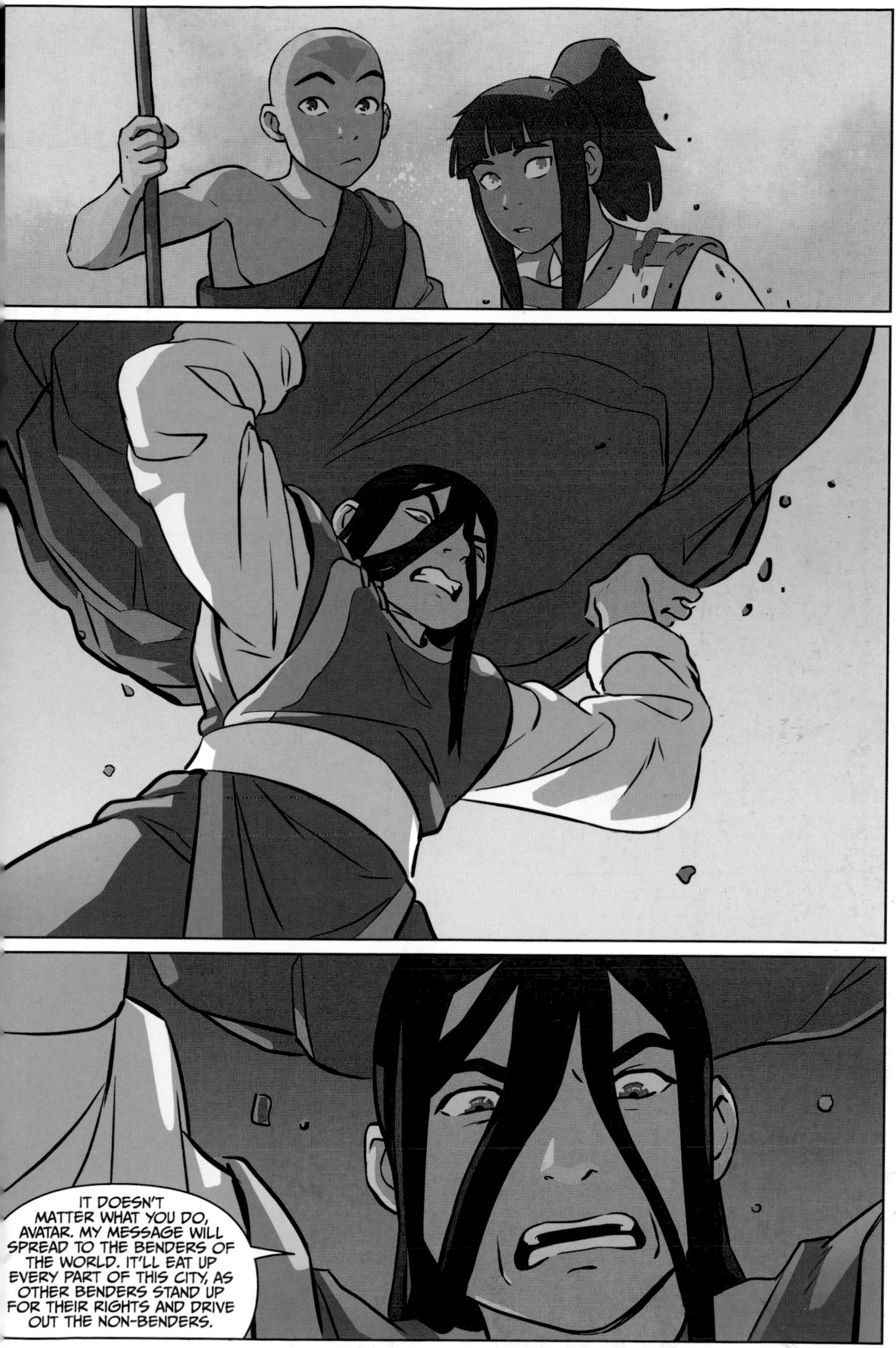
IT DOESN'T MATTER WHAT YOU DO, AVATAR. MY MESSAGE WILL SPREAD TO THE BENDERS OF THE WORLD. IT'LL EAT UP EVERY PART OF THIS CITY, AS OTHER BENDERS STAND UP FOR THEIR RIGHTS AND DRIVE OUT THE NON-BENDERS.

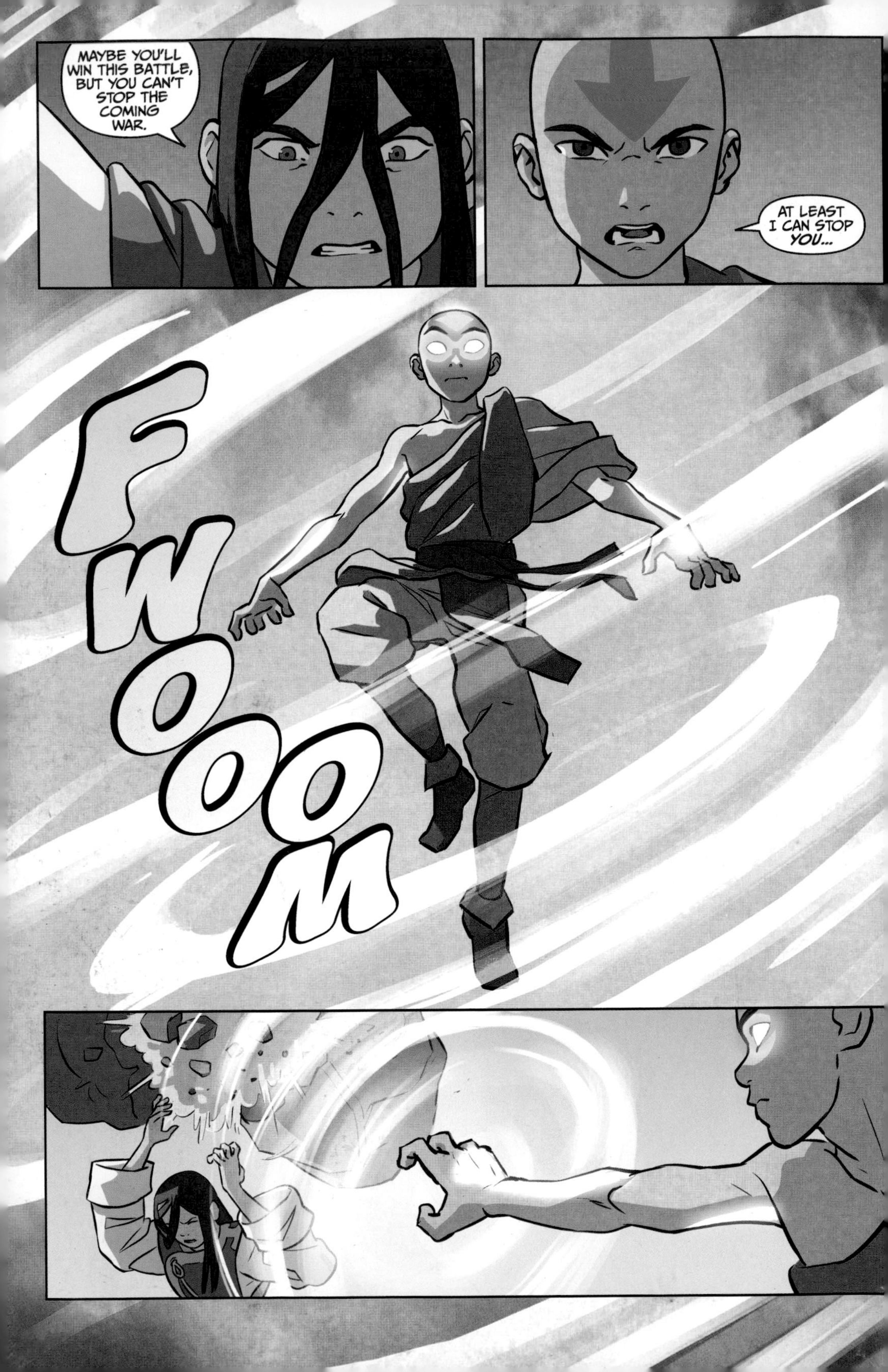
MAYBE YOU'LL WIN THIS BATTLE, BUT YOU CAN'T STOP THE COMING WAR.
AT LEAST I CAN STOP *YOU*...
FWOOOM

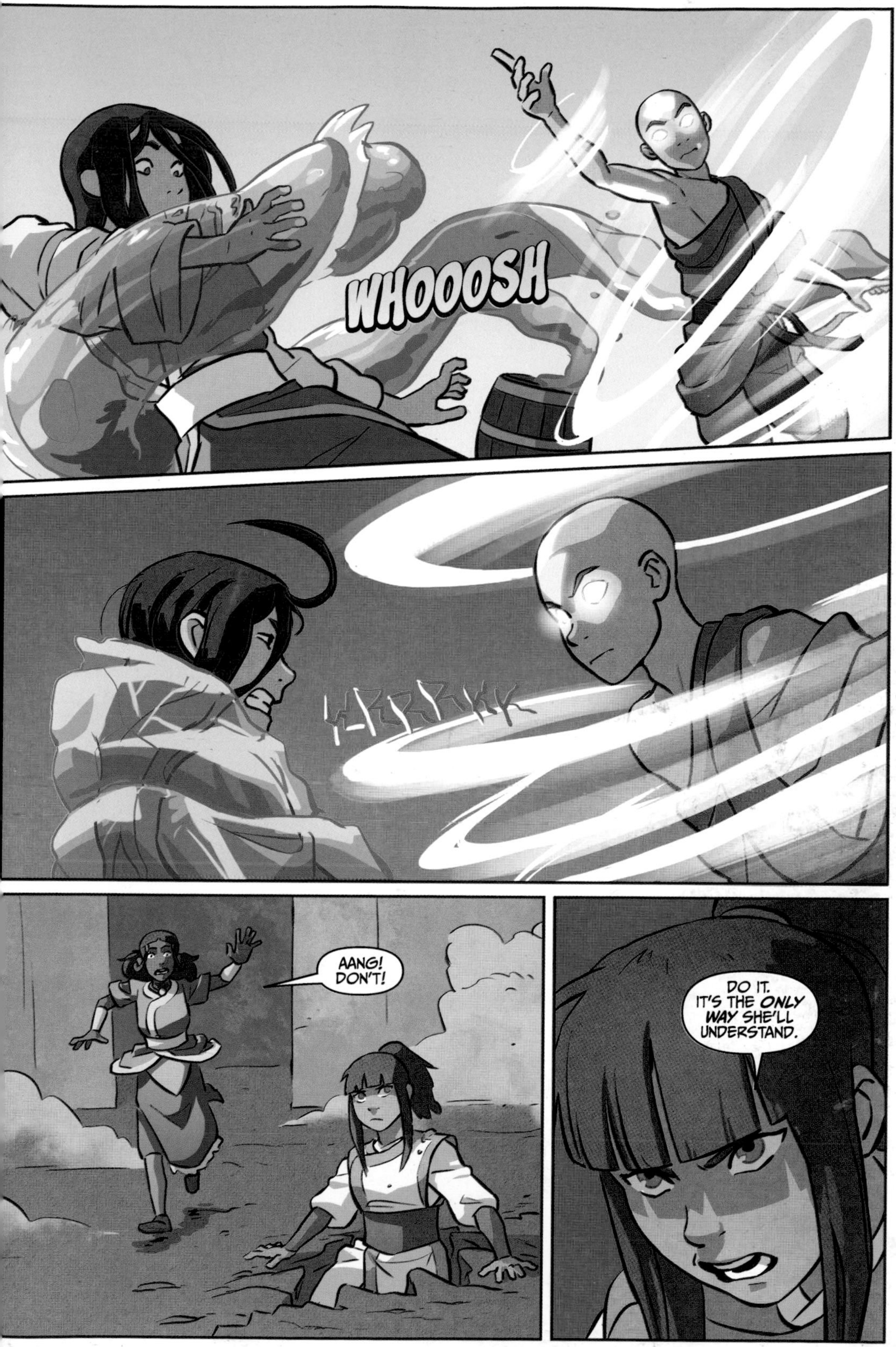
WHOOOSH
KRRRKK
AANG! DON'T!
DO IT. IT'S THE *ONLY* *WAY* SHE'LL UNDERSTAND.

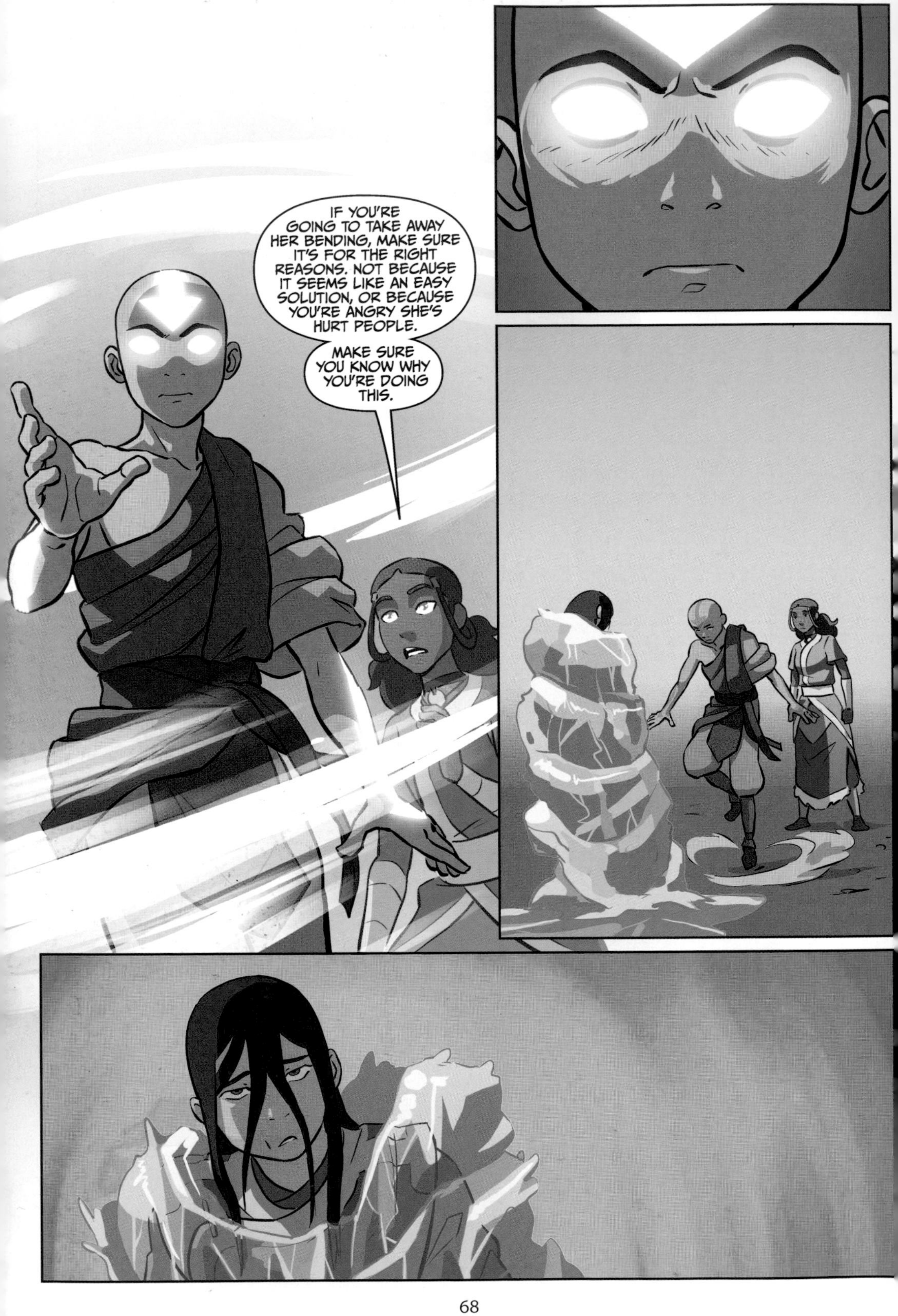
IF YOU'RE GOING TO TAKE AWAY HER BENDING, MAKE SURE IT'S FOR THE RIGHT REASONS. NOT BECAUSE IT SEEMS LIKE AN EASY SOLUTION, OR BECAUSE YOU'RE ANGRY SHE'S HURT PEOPLE.
MAKE SURE YOU KNOW WHY YOU'RE DOING THIS.

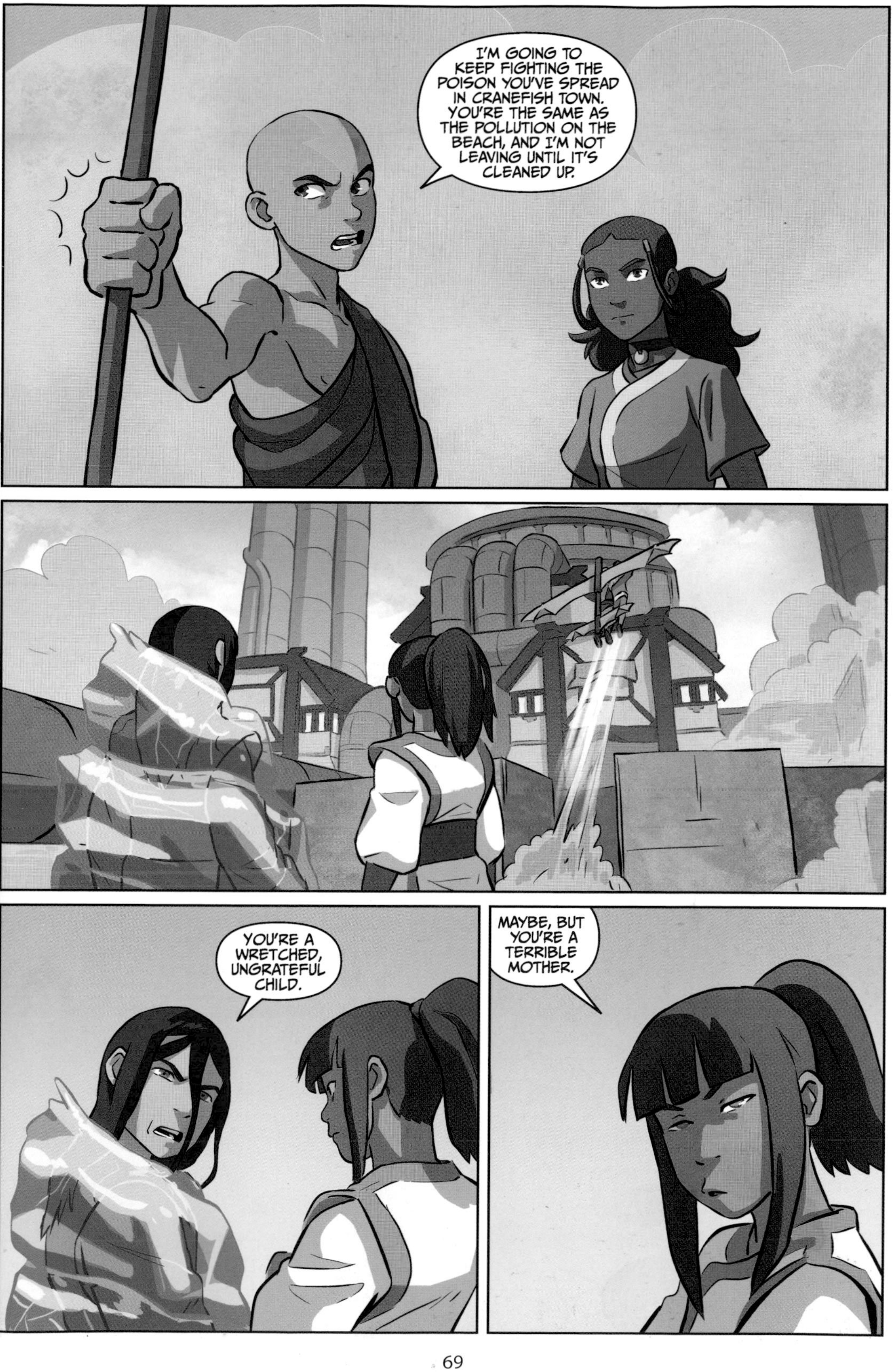
I'M GOING TO KEEP FIGHTING THE POISON YOU'VE SPREAD IN CRANEFISH TOWN. YOU'RE THE SAME AS THE POLLUTION ON THE BEACH, AND I'M NOT LEAVING UNTIL IT'S CLEANED UP.
YOU'RE A WRETCHED, UNGRATEFUL CHILD.
MAYBE, BUT YOU'RE A TERRIBLE MOTHER.

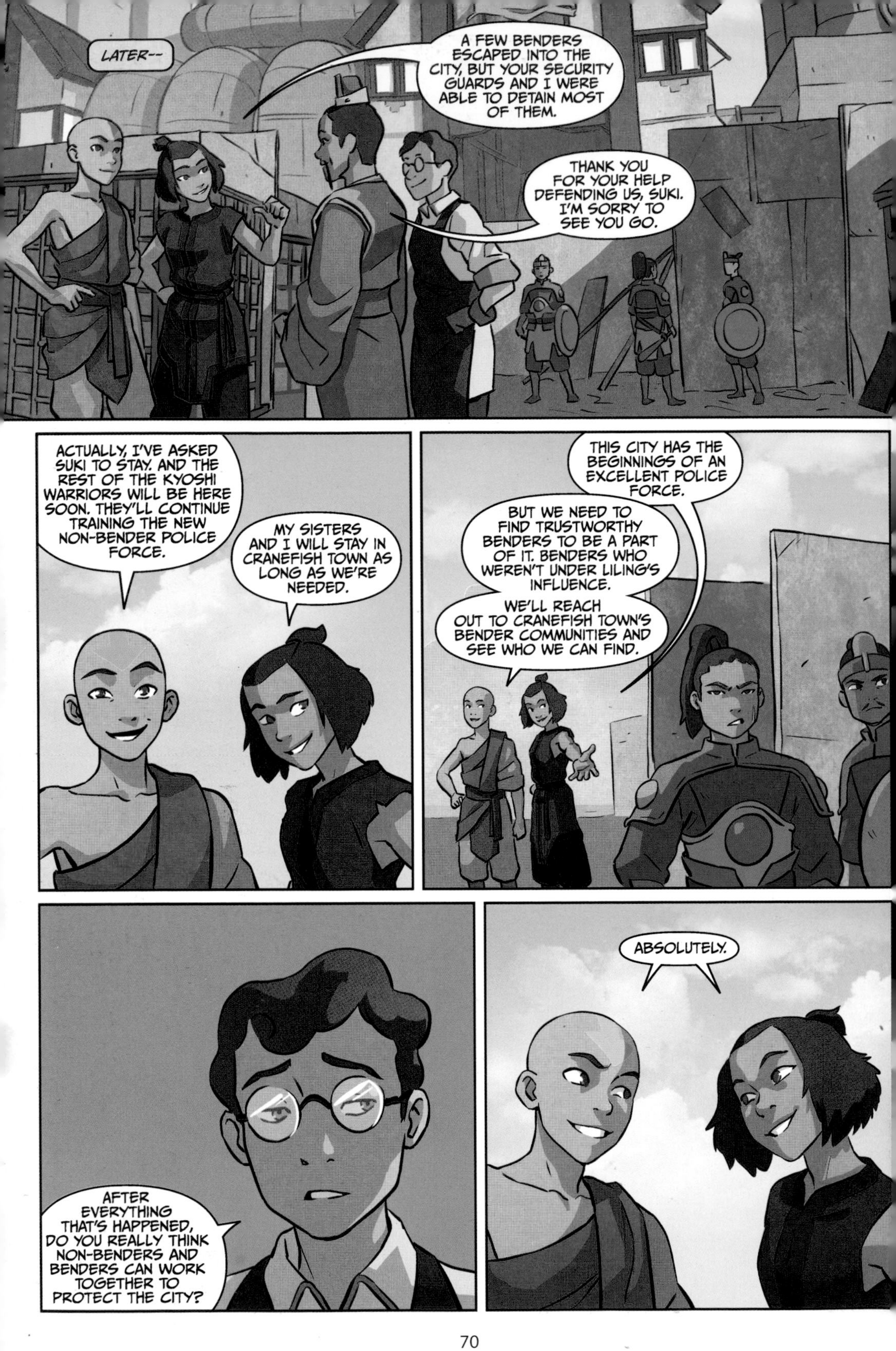
LATER--
A FEW BENDERS ESCAPED INTO THE CITY, BUT YOUR SECURITY GUARDS AND I WERE ABLE TO DETAIN MOST OF THEM.
THANK YOU FOR YOUR HELP DEFENDING US, SUKI. I'M SORRY TO SEE YOU GO.
ACTUALLY, I'VE ASKED SUKI TO STAY. AND THE REST OF THE KYOSHI WARRIORS WILL BE HERE SOON. THEY'LL CONTINUE TRAINING THE NEW NON-BENDER POLICE FORCE.
MY SISTERS AND I WILL STAY IN CRANEFISH TOWN AS LONG AS WE'RE NEEDED.
THIS CITY HAS THE BEGINNINGS OF AN EXCELLENT POLICE FORCE.
BUT WE NEED TO FIND TRUSTWORTHY BENDERS TO BE A PART OF IT. BENDERS WHO WEREN'T UNDER LILING'S INFLUENCE.
WE'LL REACH OUT TO CRANEFISH TOWN'S BENDER COMMUNITIES AND SEE WHO WE CAN FIND.
AFTER EVERYTHING THAT'S HAPPENED, DO YOU REALLY THINK NON-BENDERS AND BENDERS CAN WORK TOGETHER TO PROTECT THE CITY?
ABSOLUTELY.

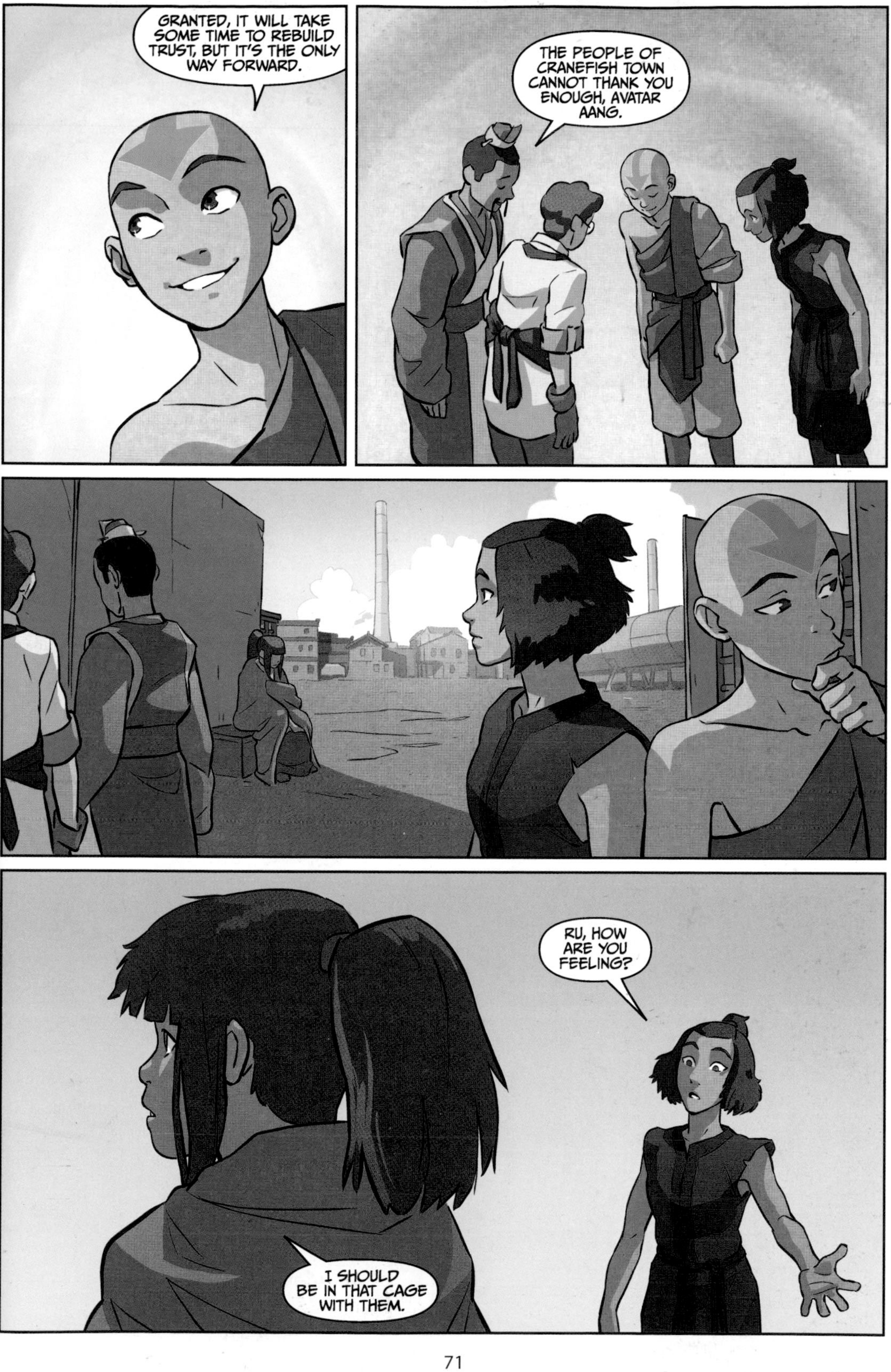
GRANTED, IT WILL TAKE SOME TIME TO REBUILD TRUST, BUT IT'S THE ONLY WAY FORWARD.
THE PEOPLE OF CRANEFISH TOWN CANNOT THANK YOU ENOUGH, AVATAR AANG.
RU, HOW ARE YOU FEELING?
I SHOULD BE IN THAT CAGE WITH THEM.

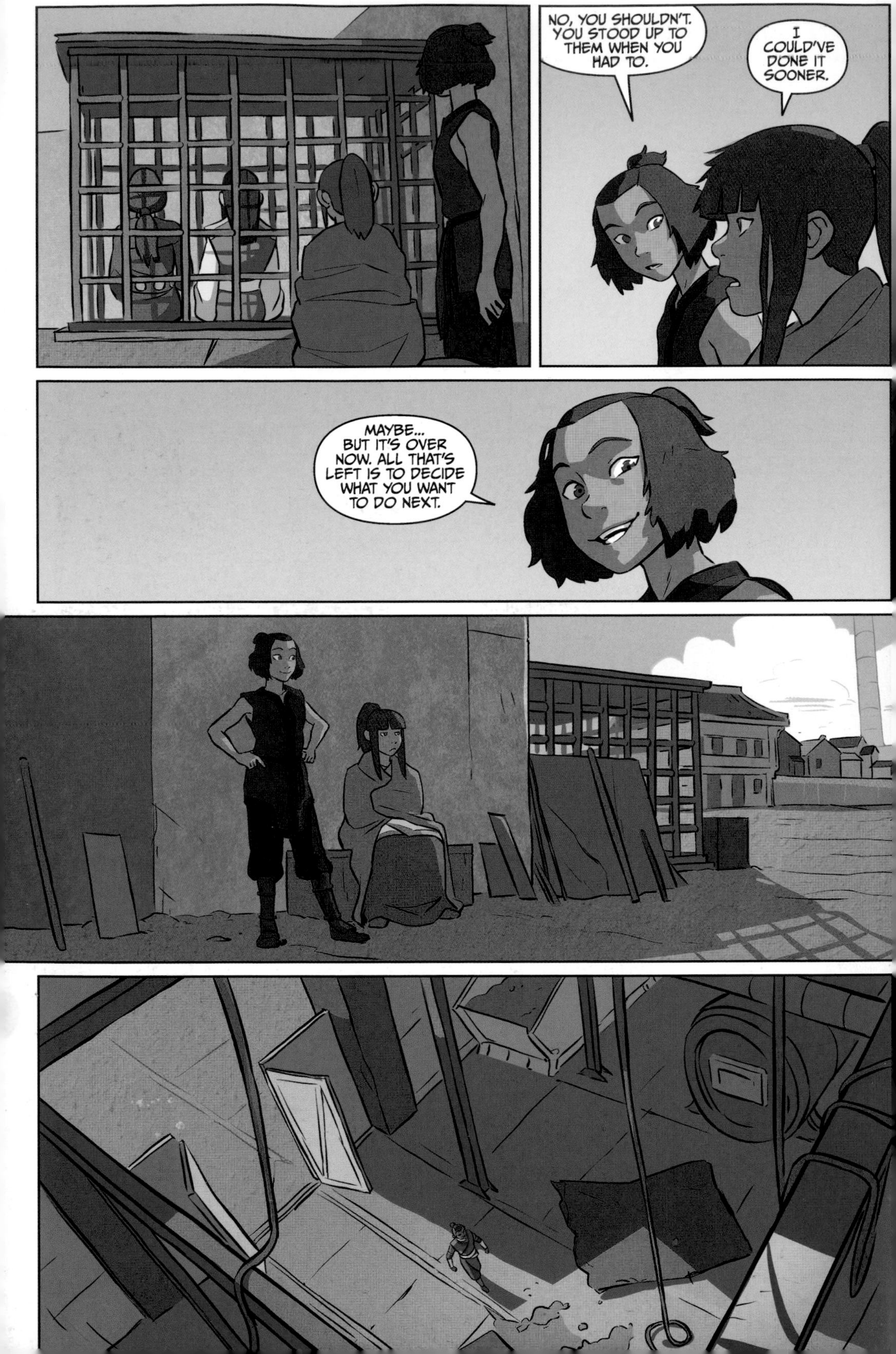
NO, YOU SHOULDN'T. YOU STOOD UP TO THEM WHEN YOU HAD TO.
I COULD'VE DONE IT SOONER.
MAYBE... BUT IT'S OVER NOW. ALL THAT'S LEFT IS TO DECIDE WHAT YOU WANT TO DO NEXT.

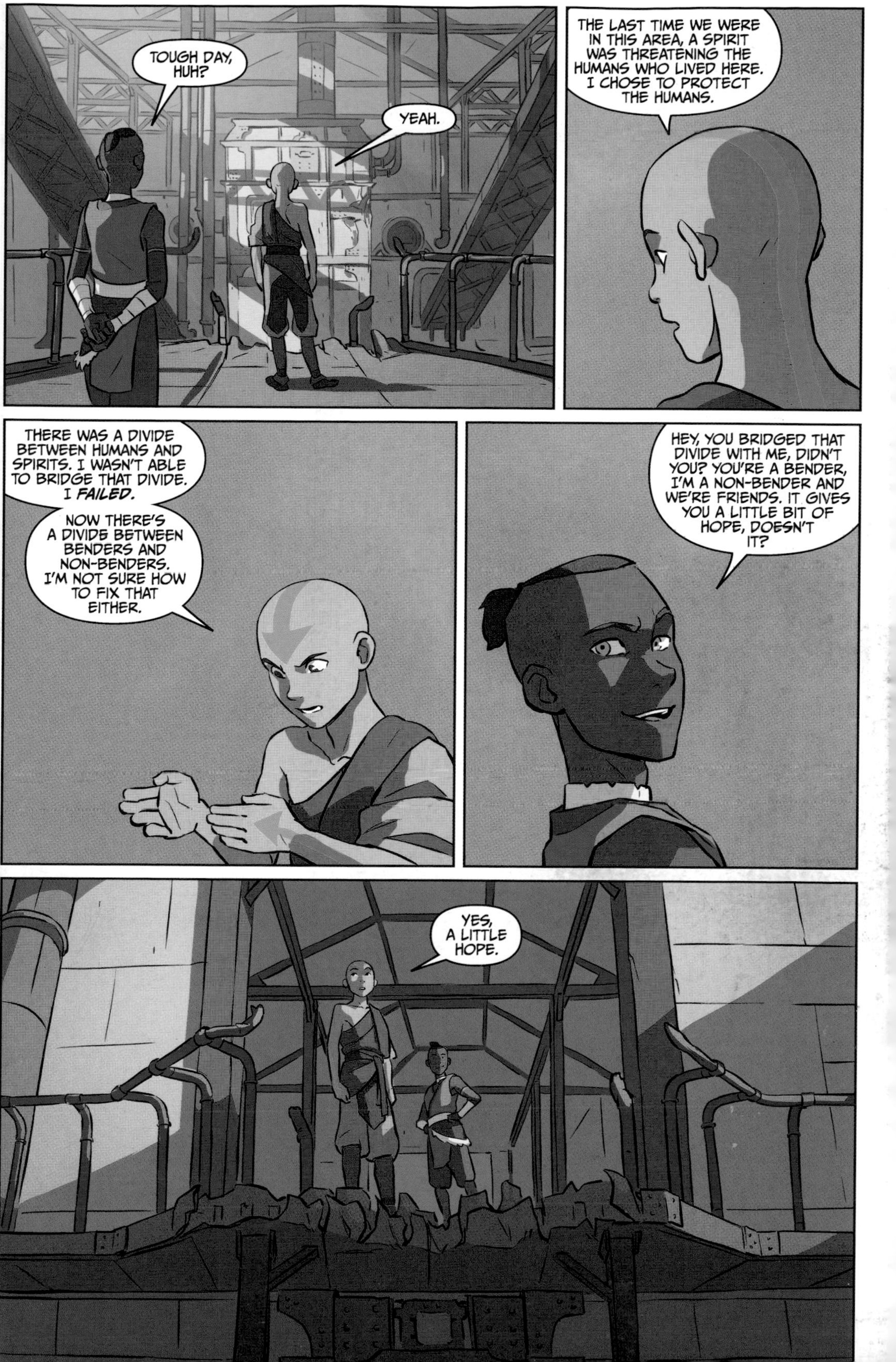
TOUGH DAY, HUH?
YEAH.
THE LAST TIME WE WERE IN THIS AREA, A SPIRIT WAS THREATENING THE HUMANS WHO LIVED HERE. I CHOSE TO PROTECT THE HUMANS.
THERE WAS A DIVIDE BETWEEN HUMANS AND SPIRITS. I WASN'T ABLE TO BRIDGE THAT DIVIDE. I FAILED.
NOW THERE'S A DIVIDE BETWEEN BENDERS AND NON-BENDERS. I'M NOT SURE HOW TO FIX THAT EITHER.
HEY, YOU BRIDGED THAT DIVIDE WITH ME, DIDN'T YOU? YOU'RE A BENDER, I'M A NON-BENDER AND WE'RE FRIENDS. IT GIVES YOU A LITTLE BIT OF HOPE, DOESN'T IT?
YES, A LITTLE HOPE.

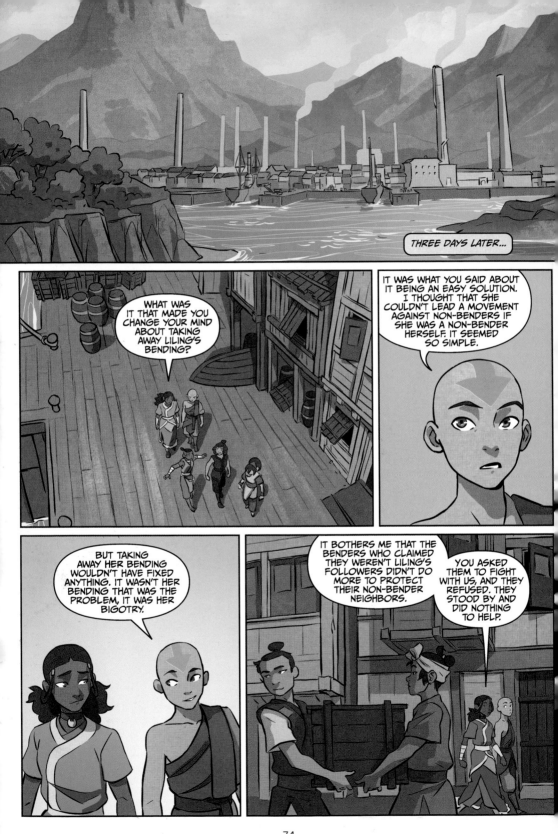

THREE DAYS LATER...

WHAT WAS IT THAT MADE YOU CHANGE YOUR MIND ABOUT TAKING AWAY LILING'S BENDING?

IT WAS WHAT YOU SAID ABOUT IT BEING AN EASY SOLUTION. I THOUGHT THAT SHE COULDN'T LEAD A MOVEMENT AGAINST NON-BENDERS IF SHE WAS A NON-BENDER HERSELF. IT SEEMED SO SIMPLE.

BUT TAKING AWAY HER BENDING WOULDN'T HAVE FIXED ANYTHING. IT WASN'T HER BENDING THAT WAS THE PROBLEM, IT WAS HER BIGOTRY.

IT BOTHERS ME THAT THE BENDERS WHO CLAIMED THEY WEREN'T LILING'S FOLLOWERS DIDN'T DO MORE TO PROTECT THEIR NON-BENDER NEIGHBORS.

YOU ASKED THEM TO FIGHT WITH US, AND THEY REFUSED. THEY STOOD BY AND DID NOTHING TO HELP.

74

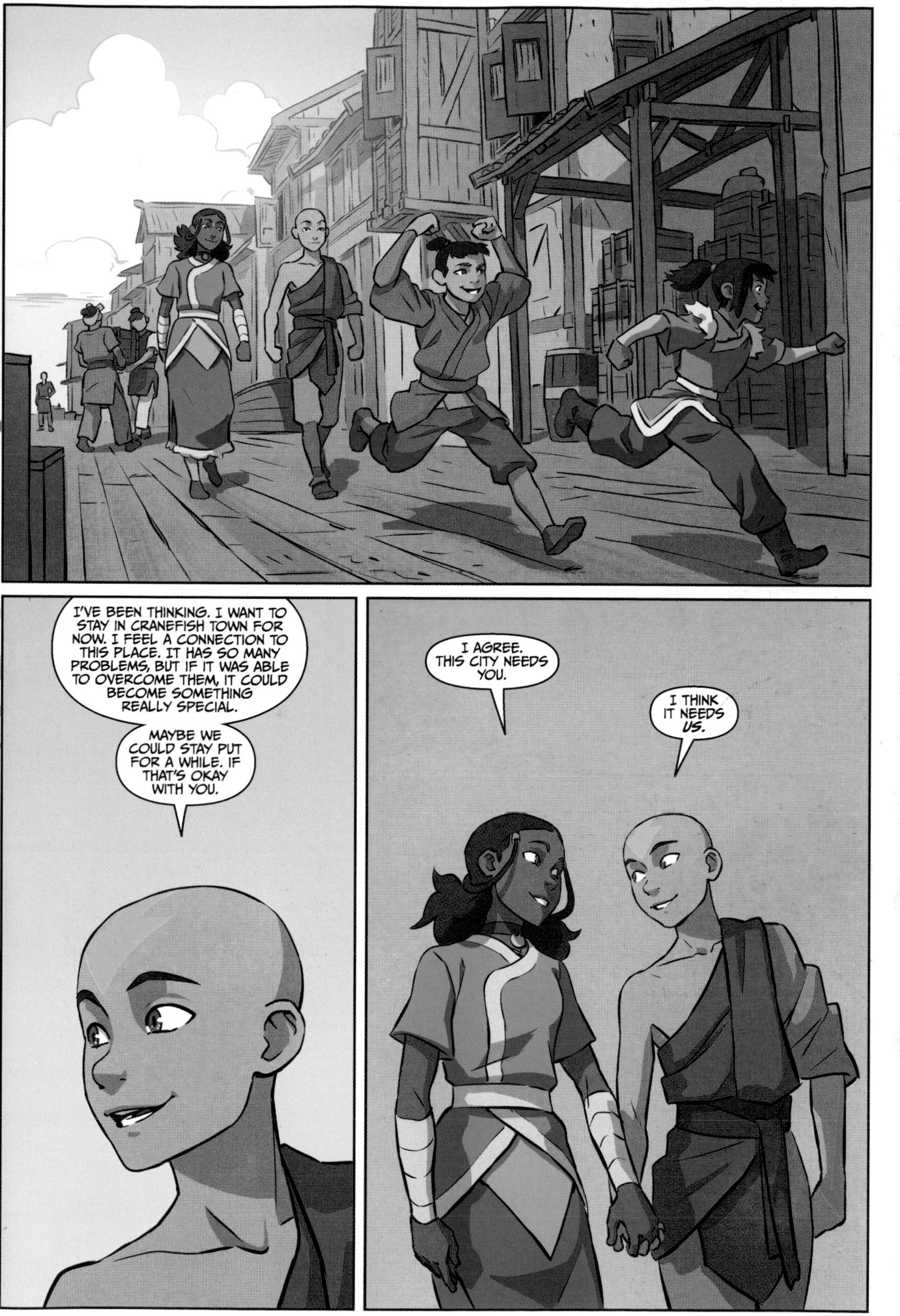
I'VE BEEN THINKING. I WANT TO STAY IN CRANEFISH TOWN FOR NOW. I FEEL A CONNECTION TO THIS PLACE. IT HAS SO MANY PROBLEMS, BUT IF IT WAS ABLE TO OVERCOME THEM, IT COULD BECOME SOMETHING REALLY SPECIAL.
MAYBE WE COULD STAY PUT FOR A WHILE. IF THAT'S OKAY WITH YOU.
I AGREE. THIS CITY NEEDS YOU.
I THINK IT NEEDS *US.*

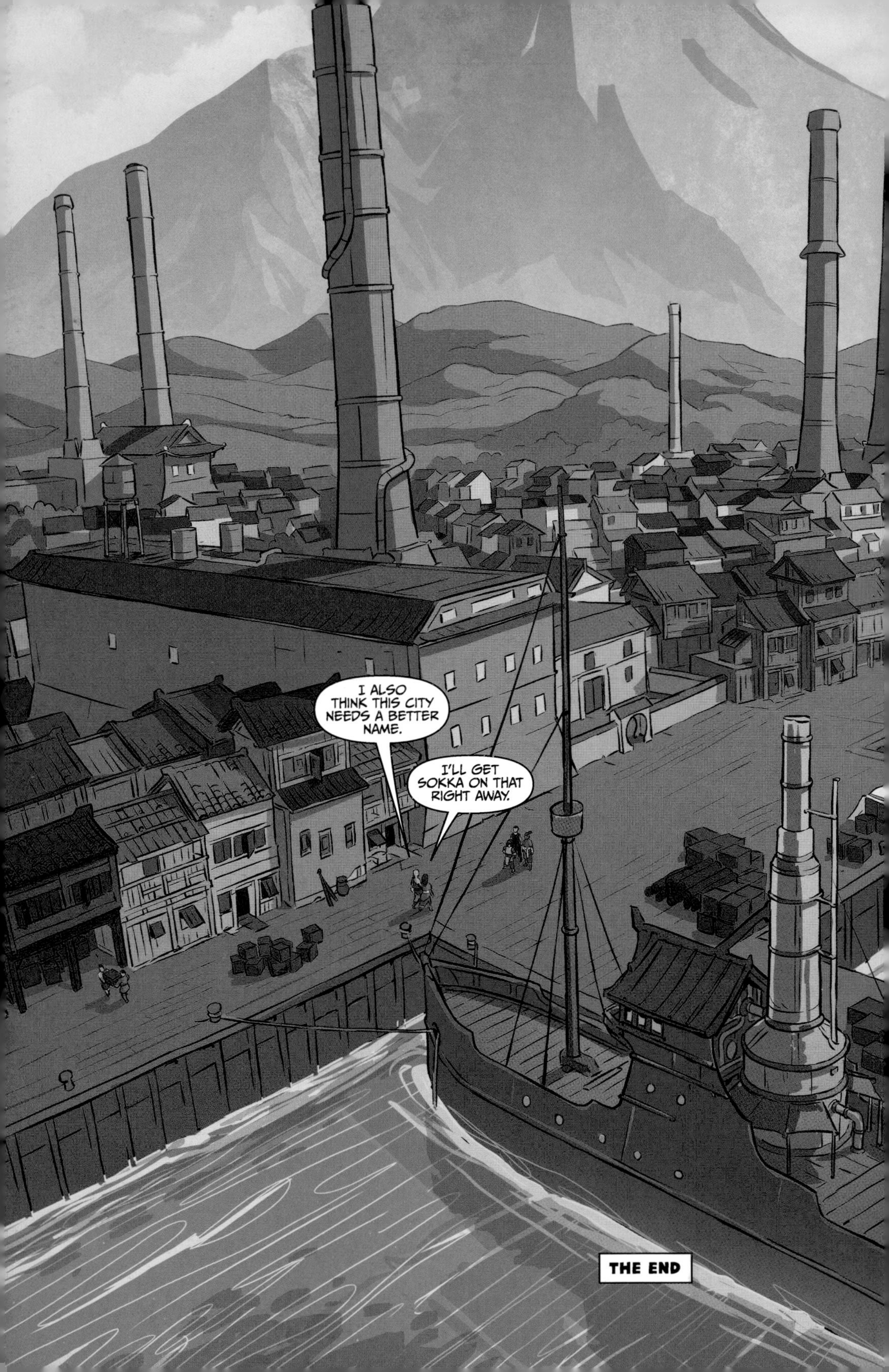
I ALSO THINK THIS CITY NEEDS A BETTER NAME.
I'LL GET SOKKA ON THAT RIGHT AWAY.
THE END

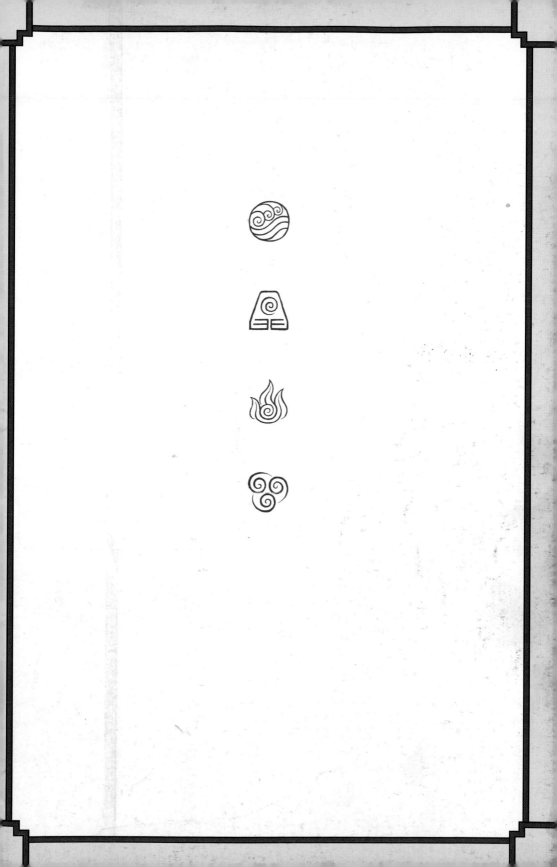

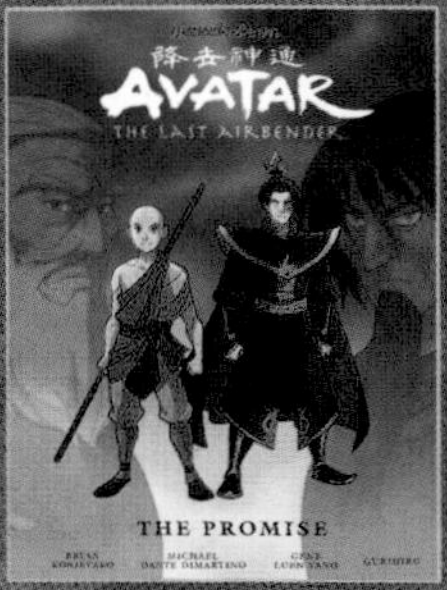
nickelodeon
AVATAR
THE LAST AIRBENDER
THE PROMISE

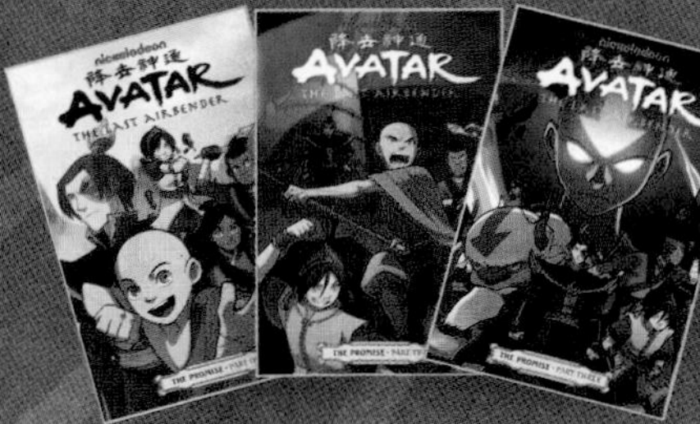
nickelodeon
AVATAR
THE LAST AIRBENDER

Avatar: The Last Airbender—The Promise Library Edition
978-1-61655-074-5 $39.99

Avatar: The Last Airbender—The Promise Part 1
978-1-59582-811-8 $10.99

Avatar: The Last Airbender—The Promise Part 2
978-1-59582-875-0 $10.99

Avatar: The Last Airbender—The Promise Part 3
978-1-59582-941-2 $10.99

Avatar: The Last Airbender—The Search Library Edition
978-1-61655-226-8 $39.99

Avatar: The Last Airbender—The Search Part 1
978-1-61655-054-7 $10.99

Avatar: The Last Airbender—The Search Part 2
978-1-61655-190-2 $10.99

Avatar: The Last Airbender—The Search Part 3
978-1-61655-184-1 $10.99

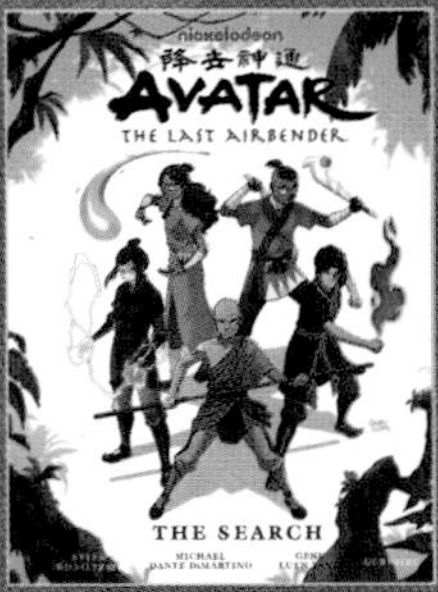
nickelodeon
AVATAR
THE LAST AIRBENDER
THE SEARCH

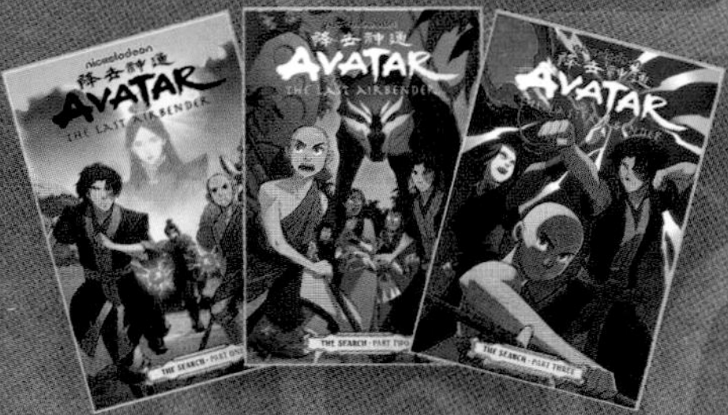
nickelodeon
AVATAR
THE LAST AIRBENDER

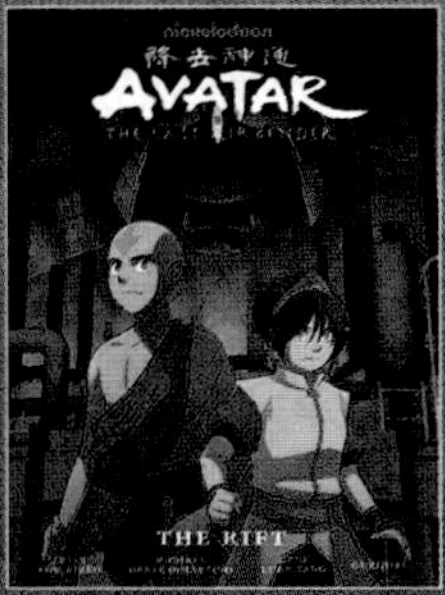
nickelodeon
AVATAR
THE RIFT

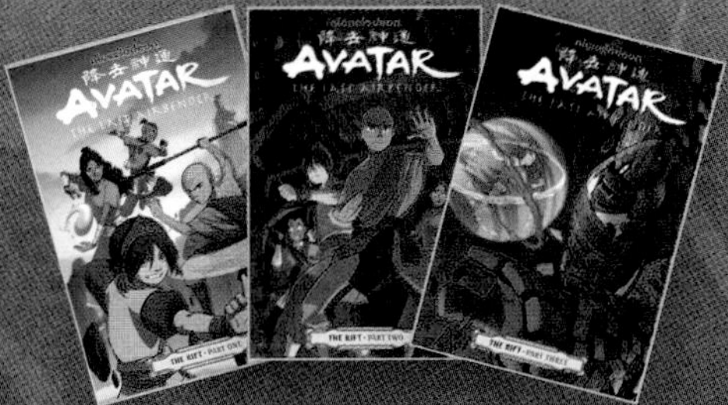
nickelodeon
AVATAR
THE LAST AIRBENDER

Avatar: The Last Airbender—The Rift Library Edition
978-1-61655-550-4 $39.99

Avatar: The Last Airbender—The Rift Part 1
978-1-61655-295-4 $10.99

Avatar: The Last Airbender—The Rift Part 2
978-1-61655-296-1 $10.99

Avatar: The Last Airbender—The Rift Part 3
978-1-61655-297-8 $10.99

Avatar: The Last Airbender—Smoke and Shadow Library Edition
978-1-50670-013-7 $39.99

Avatar: The Last Airbender—Smoke and Shadow Part 1
978-1-61655-761-4 $10.99

Avatar: The Last Airbender—Smoke and Shadow Part 2
978-1-61655-790-4 $10.99

Avatar: The Last Airbender—Smoke and Shadow Part 3
978-1-61655-838-3 $10.99

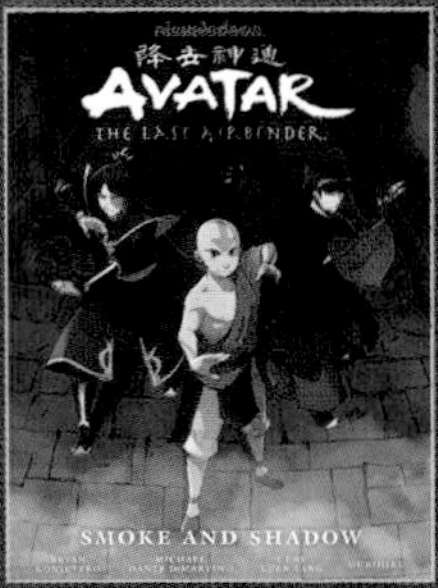
nickelodeon
AVATAR
THE LAST AIRBENDER
SMOKE AND SHADOW

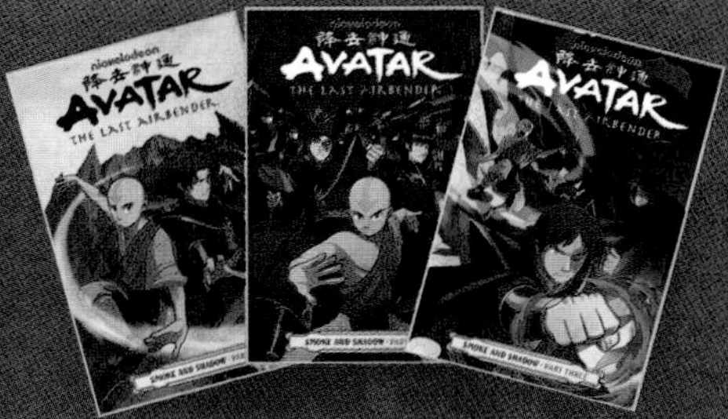
nickelodeon
AVATAR
THE LAST AIRBENDER

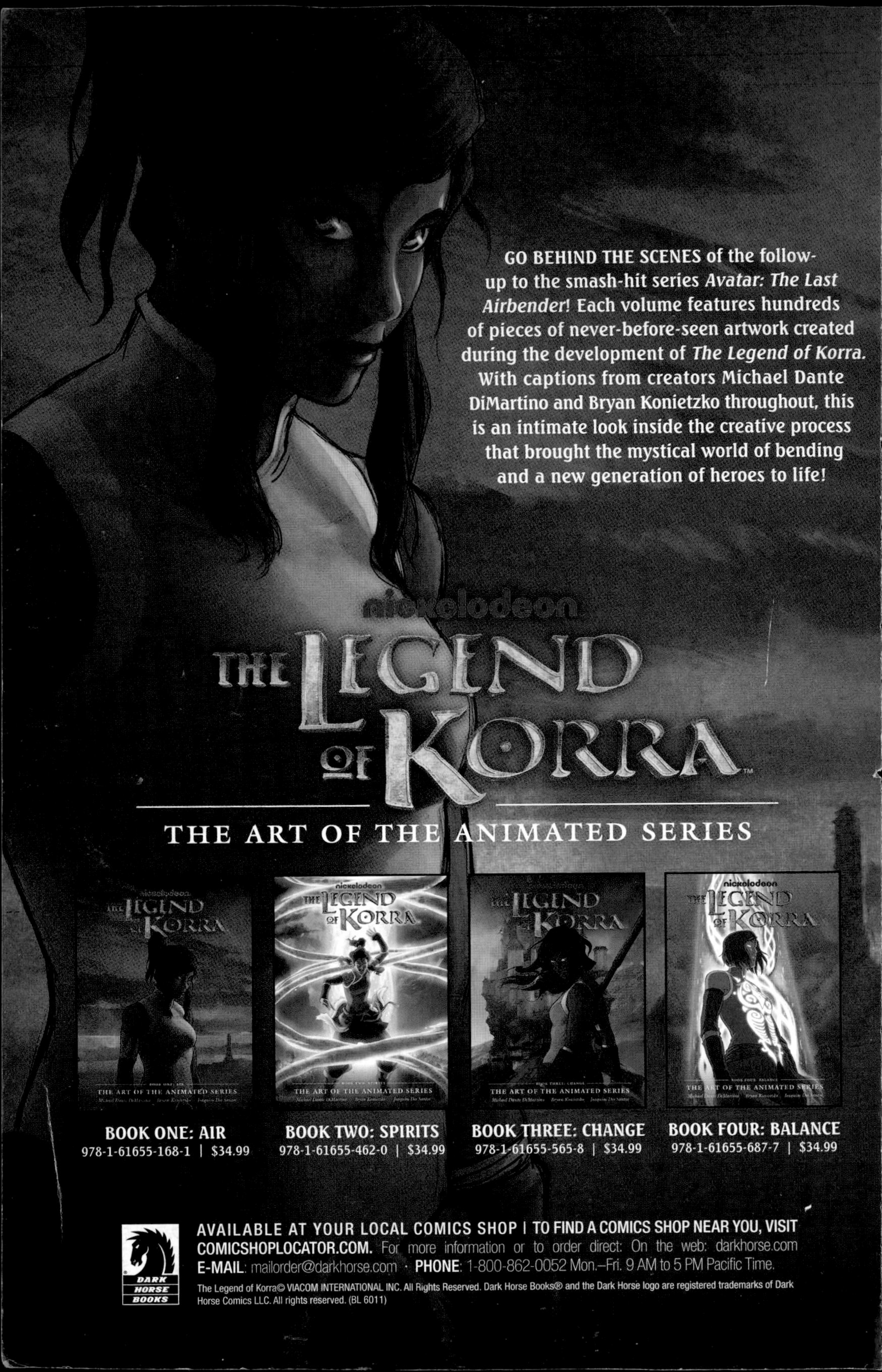
GO BEHIND THE SCENES of the follow-up to the smash-hit series *Avatar: The Last Airbender*! Each volume features hundreds of pieces of never-before-seen artwork created during the development of *The Legend of Korra*. With captions from creators Michael Dante DiMartino and Bryan Konietzko throughout, this is an intimate look inside the creative process that brought the mystical world of bending and a new generation of heroes to life!
nickelodeon
THE LEGEND OF KORRA™
THE ART OF THE ANIMATED SERIES
BOOK ONE: AIR
978-1-61655-168-1 | $34.99
BOOK TWO: SPIRITS
978-1-61655-462-0 | $34.99
BOOK THREE: CHANGE
978-1-61655-565-8 | $34.99
BOOK FOUR: BALANCE
978-1-61655-687-7 | $34.99
DARK HORSE BOOKS
AVAILABLE AT YOUR LOCAL COMICS SHOP | TO FIND A COMICS SHOP NEAR YOU, VISIT COMICSHOPLOCATOR.COM. For more information or to order direct: On the web: darkhorse.com
E-MAIL: mailorder@darkhorse.com · PHONE: 1-800-862-0052 Mon.–Fri. 9 AM to 5 PM Pacific Time.
The Legend of Korra© VIACOM INTERNATIONAL INC. All Rights Reserved. Dark Horse Books® and the Dark Horse logo are registered trademarks of Dark Horse Comics LLC. All rights reserved. (BL 6011)